THE
INDUSTRIAL
(MARKETING)
REVOLUTION

THE
INDUSTRIAL
(MARKETING)
REVOLUTION

HOW TECHNOLOGY CHANGES EVERYTHING
FOR THE INDUSTRIAL MARKETER

JARED R. FABAC

iUniverse LLC
Bloomington

The Industrial (Marketing) Revolution
How Technology Changes Everything for the Industrial Marketer

iUniverse books may be ordered through booksellers or by contacting:

iUniverse LLC
1663 Liberty Drive
Bloomington, IN 47403
www.iuniverse.com
1-800-Authors (1-800-288-4677)

ISBN: 978-1-4759-9847-4 (sc)
ISBN: 978-1-4759-9848-1 (hc)
ISBN: 978-1-4759-9849-8 (ebk)

Library of Congress Control Number: 2013912544

Printed in the United States of America

iUniverse rev. date: 07/11/2013

CONTENTS

Part 4: The Final Conversion—Creating Customers

INTRODUCTION

If you're reading this book, then chances are good that you are ready for a *revolution*—a revolution of thoughts, of ideas, of how you operate the "marketing machinery" that drives leads, prospects, customers, and sales to your industrial company.

Many marketing, SEO, and social media books offer steps, solutions, strategies, and secrets—whatever the "expert" authors call them—but most marketing books *fail for our industry* because they *fail to take our industry into account.*

This one doesn't; it's industry born and industry specific. I am the founder and director of strategy of Idea Bright Marketing (www.ideabrightmarketing.com), an industrial marketing agency specializing in digital media.

The Birth of Lean Marketing

It all began in 2006 while I was working as an industrial business consultant for the Small Business Development Center at Gannon University. I had a unique opportunity to work with many industrial companies, from start-up manufacturers to large, multimillion-dollar corporations. I spent my time racing through business development platforms that explored the traditional methods of marketing in the industrial atmosphere. I was consumed by analyzing companies from a data-driven standpoint that drowned me in their environments.

In many cases, thanks to my ongoing analysis and the demand of our client base, I became more knowledgeable about the industrial markets than the largest players themselves. As the economy took a turn for the worse in 2008, I had the opportunity to work with companies as they defined turnaround-marketing strategies to recover. In the same year, I personally developed twenty turnaround strategies for industrial companies.

During that time, I was able to identify and adjust to the fact that buying power was shifting drastically from the vendor to the buyer—based on the ability to utilize the web to streamline purchasing decisions. This led directly to the creation of Idea Bright Marketing, which would be focused on developing technology and services to transition the industrial community to a modern age of marketing by utilizing concepts already familiar to the industry.

Lean marketing, which is explained thoroughly in this book, was introduced, and it positioned industrial companies to expand market reach, grow lead generation, and operate more efficiently from a sales perspective than ever before.

It is an exciting time to be an industrial marketer. Over the past few years, traditional methods of business development have been fundamentally breaking down, falling apart, becoming irrelevant, or disappearing altogether. Market share that was once dominated by a select few is openly accessible; the sooner you adapt to these principles, the faster you can position yourself as an industry leader.

Revolutionize Your Marketing Platform to Drive New Business

I'm blessed that in my current position, I have the opportunity to dedicate my life to helping companies like yours—engineering, technical, industrial, and manufacturing professionals—revolutionize their marketing platforms to drive new business.

Many marketing agencies work for all comers; we've intentionally avoided that. We stick to what we know because it's such a specialized field; frankly, few people know you the way we know you.

We don't help companies sell shoes; we help the companies that produce the metal eyelets to protect shoelaces increase their business and sell more units. We don't help companies sell microwaves; we help the companies who provide the digital circuitry inside the microwaves sell more units. You get the point.

We are invested in this industry because you are what makes the world go round. The more the world changes, the more the world stays the same; your products—and the products they produce—are more in demand than ever.

And, yet, you are in crisis mode. You're faced with offshore competition. What used to work, no longer does—or it doesn't work as effectively. What has always sold more widgets, wires, machines, steel, and chrome is failing you; that's why you're reading this book.

It's not your fault—and you haven't failed. This is new. The majority of our clients are working hard and hiring expertly creative marketers to increase visibility, solidify brand, and drive qualified leads to the sales department. The problem is that the way people buy has changed, but you haven't.

The (New) Industrial Revolution

During the Industrial Revolution, change came at a lightning pace. Maybe it doesn't seem that way looking back; to our eyes, the old Ford factories, textile mills, and production lines at the turn of the twentieth century can seem downright archaic.

But imagine the farmers, business owners, entrepreneurs, and machinists who had to come in from the fields or put down their looms to sit at a painfully dizzying machine for nine or ten hours a day, six days a week.

Switching from standing to sitting was a revolution for many people, to say nothing of moving hearth and home from the rural to the urban environment. In the blink of an eye, life as they knew it—life as we knew it, life as the country, and even how the world knew it—had changed forever.

Those who resisted the change lost more than their jobs or their livelihoods; they lost valuable and game-changing *momentum*. Opportunity comes to those who see potential and act on it, not those who cross their arms and lament change until it passes them by.

Every revolution has its naysayers, doubters, and grumps. People once thought cars would never replace horses, radios would never replace live performance, TVs would never replace radios, and phones were a luxury item that few would embrace.

Today those products are even enhanced with TV-DVR, satellite radio, and mobile communications that give the user more power to determine how they are marketed—and how they are not. Commercials are skipped or fast-forwarded through while watching on alternate media. Radio advertising has been passed over in favor of subscriber channels, and direct mailing is non-existent on electronic devices.

You hear the same cries echoing throughout today's most vocal, and conservative, pundits; those who fight e-books even as Kindles and Nooks show up under every Christmas tree, those who continue to embrace CDs even as music downloads, iTunes, and iPods become the new standard in music appreciation, and those who continue to harness direct mailing and complain about junk mail.

But nowhere is clinging to the old ways of doing things more harmful to industrial companies than by embracing the traditional advertising media of old. Print ads, direct mail, print catalogs and directories, trade journals, and trade shows. For decades, for generations really, these traditional marketing strategies have been the backbone of growth for our industry, just as the library was the backbone to research.

Once upon a time, buyers wanted to hold a widget, bend a wire, or even shake a hand—and many still will. Those traditional marketing tools still have relevance for today's B2B customers; this isn't about throwing the baby out with the bathwater. However, the industrial company that denies the other half of the marketing equation—technology, web, and social media marketing—is the modern equivalent of driving a horse and buggy on the freeway.

Face the Facts, Face the Future

This book is about facing facts; it's about recognizing the value of traditional versus modern, technological media—websites, e-mail marketing, search engine optimization, online directories, webinars, and the like—and defining a unique "media mix" that works for you.

The Industrial Revolution forever changed the way we produced, bought, sold, and consumed modern goods. Today we are in a second, even more precarious Industrial Marketing Revolution that is likewise changing how we decide which companies to use, which products to buy, who to buy them from, which brands to be loyal to, and even which CEOs are worthy—personally and professionally—of our business.

This new industrial revolution is not about the failure of your product, your customer service, or your marketing department; this revolution is about content. No one is asking you to produce more, cut costs, hire new people or give up on the forms of advertising that still work for you.

I am asking you to open the bay doors to the idea that content—articles, white papers, blogs, websites, e-catalogs—is driving sales, now more than ever. This book explains how to produce content that aligns with your products and marketplace—while making people associate you with both.

Parting Words about the Industrial Marketing Revolution: *Embracing Technology from the Ground Up*

Revolution equals change, plain and simple. Change can be painful. Every day, I'm talk to companies about change, and I can see the reluctance on their faces even as I promise to dedicate myself to revolutionizing the way they reach, sell, and close new—and more—customers.

You don't want to change; I get that, too. The problem is that *you have to change*. Not just to keep up, not just to thrive and grow, but to survive, you must change how you market to address the technology that is forcing you and your competitors to evolve at lightning speed. If you don't, they will.

Together, we can make this *Industrial Marketing Revolution*, if not exactly painless, then at least *simple, predictable,* and *repeatable.* In this book, you will find answers for many of your questions—spelled out succinctly and with solutions for every pain point.

SEO? I've got you covered.

Web design? I've got your back.

Blogging? Don't worry; I'll spell it out for you.

Social media? You've come to the right place.

And everything in between.

Technology isn't going anywhere, and if you ignore it, neither will you—or your company. The only way to make effective use of your marketing people—and bridge their efforts with sales and capture the profit stream that awaits—is to not just address technology, but *embrace it.*

PART
1

The Industrial Marketing Revolution

CHAPTER 1

Lead, Follow, or Show Us the Way—The Death of Traditional Marketing

Imagine what it must have felt like to early factory owners at the onset of the Industrial Revolution. To watch production exponentially explode overnight, to have all your employees gathered in one location versus piecemeal all over town, to set standards for quality, and meet those standards with direct supervision—all under one roof. To set higher standards and meet stiffer deadlines and increase market share by market dominance.

Much like the Industrial Revolution forever changed the way manufacturers produced goods, the Internet has completely and irrevocably changed the way we produce something even more important to modern consumers: *information.*

The web has not altered the marketing landscape simply because we're all addicted to the buzz and hum of modern technology. Instead, society is becoming increasingly addicted to technology and, thus, the Internet because it is the quickest, most effective, and simplest form of *gathering information* to make more informed decisions about available products.

All marketing is information—and every development since the Internet came into the marketing vernacular—is another step toward more information, easier and faster. The Internet provides more information about you, your company, your brand, your products, your services, and your success.

3

If we look more closely at traditional industrial advertising, we can see that it, too, was an early means of research:

- **Trade shows**: For decades, trade shows were a leading source of information for B2B consumers and, quite often, the first leg of a fact-finding tour that led them straight to a particular product and/or vendor. Today the Internet is playing that role more than ever. It is now a live, 24/7 trade show where those in need can find your products and fully evaluate them before making a purchase.
- **Direct mail**: Brochures, catalogs, and other pieces of direct mail let potential buyers learn valuable information about your products in the most attractive, modern manner possible. Now we call that a website; rather than remaining on the printed page, product descriptions and images are becoming fully interactive by integrating specifications with product overviews. Websites are also giving users the ability to quickly source specific products without having to surf through hundreds of pages.
- **Trade journals**: Appearing in a trade journal gave industrial marketers a wide, targeted audience for their product, be it in print advertising or being featured in an article or editorial. Blogs, white papers, e-books, and other editorial—and original—content are quickly replacing the slower, limited editorial pace and space of trade journals. Content is no longer an appealing accommodation to products; it is a necessity expected by the sourcing end users.

Research Redirected

If you look at all marketing as some form of research in a sales-driven cycle, it should come as no surprise that speed (through faster access to information through the web) beats tradition every time. In the past, buyers seeking industrial products followed a set pattern of research and fact-finding before spending their company's money. Generally speaking, they pored through printed material (catalogs, brochures, and trade journals). They queried colleagues and coworkers about Company A's widgets or Company B's wires, adding word of mouth and personal referrals to the data they'd already gathered in print. At a certain point, they would call your toll-free number and begin the process of ordering from you, eventually completing the cumbersome and lengthy sales process.

Analytically speaking, modern buyers are no different from traditional ones; they have simply short-circuited the traditional method to do more research—faster and more effectively—online in order to make more accurate decisions based on their needs.

Your website—or your competitor's website—has become a veritable 24/7 trade show complete with product descriptions, photos, specifications, and possibly even reviews, endorsements, and demonstration videos. What was once only accomplished through a planned face-to-face engagement is now being accomplished faster and more efficiently than ever.

A host of resources on your blog, including white papers, special reports, and e-books provides them with "drill down" data to make better, more informed choices, faster.

Review sites, Facebook, Twitter, forums, and other social media hot spots have taken the place of "phone tag" for most buyers, and they can be performed at any time with the click of a mouse. No voice mail or phone tag is required. E-mail has become the primary form of communication in almost all industrial offices throughout the world.

The process is essentially the same: research + fact finding + peer review = buying decision. The only difference now is the speed of the process and the tools one uses to complete it.

Trade Shows and Traditional Advertising Are Suffering

According to the 2008 Tradeshow Week Exhibition Management Survey, trade show attendance dropped in excess of 25 percent.

These declines have been contributing factors in a number of national shows becoming regional—and some shows combining with others.

The trade show industry has been continuously trending downward the last few years, with a more precipitous drop late in 2008 and into Q2 of 2009. The Tradeshow Week Quarterly Report of Tradeshow Statistics reported a sharp decline in Q2 2009 in two indexes it tracks: attendance was down 10.4 percent, and the number of exhibiting companies decreased by over 13 percent. Both of these indexes showed declines from Q1 2009. Trade show statistics have been steadily decreasing ever since.

With travel budgets and in-person trade shows are on the decline, virtual trade shows—hosted completely online—are on the rise. Two major providers of trade show services report record growth this year.

The number of ad pages in printed business publications continues to plummet. Total ad pages in business-to-business (B2B) publications fell more than 30 percent in the first half of 2009 compared to the same period in 2008; some publications suffered more than 50 percent declines in ad pages.

And virtually every title tracked by Interactive Media Services showed losses of 20 percent or more in ad pages for Q1 2009 compared to Q1 2008. The subsequent loss in revenues has led to some B2B publishers to sell their print publications, but few are finding buyers. Other publications are reducing publishing frequency.

However, this decline in ad pages and revenue is not a surprising trend: due to the migration of your audience online, the printed advertising industry was struggling even before the economic recession.

A Shift toward the Future

As goes the rest of the country, so goes the industrial segment of our industry. Many general trade magazines and newspapers are slowly dying off, such as the Baltimore *Examiner* and the Rocky Mountain *News* and *Gourmet, Vibe,* and *Teen,* and so are such specialized industry publications, such as *PC Magazine, Pilot Journal,* and *Training Magazine.*

It's more than a trend or a downturn; it's a national, even global, shift in how we gather information. Print magazines, newspapers, and heavy industry trade journals and periodicals can't compete with the instant, almost real-time, flow of information that appears daily on websites, blogs, forums, and other web-based resources that supply us with the information we need to make decisions.

The lead-time for an article on a print editorial calendar can be four to six months; thanks to the Internet, the same information can appear in four or six *hours*—and certainly within four or six days.

With the rise of iPads, Kindles, Nooks, and other mobile- and tablet-driven technology, readers can get the same instantaneous content in an interactive and attractive format that closely mimics the pages, even the layouts, of print publications but in a more vibrant, dynamic, and immediate way. And they are—in droves. According to *Media Daily News,* "Out of 187 million American adults who interacted with magazine content and ads in the period covered by the AMS, 54 percent did so via the web or mobile platforms, including smartphones, eReaders, tablets, and other mobile devices."

As long as the content has quality and is relevant, it's hard to resist faster and better over just plain better.

Managing Your Media Mix

Another seismic shift to accompany the Industrial Marketing Revolution is the rapid decline of paid advertising. With On-Demand television and movies, viewers can easily fast-forward through the commercials—or avoid them altogether with subscription-based services like Netflix and Hulu.

In print media, such as magazines, trade journals, and newspapers, the new cry for industrial marketers will be their "media mix." Consumers are still reading print, but they're often accessing it online through tablets, laptops, and even cell phones.

According to Nielsen's *Connected Devices Playbook*, "On any given weekday, 70 percent of iPad owners spend at least 15 minutes with magazine content on their devices, with 33 percent spending between 31 and 60 minutes."

This media mix—the "stickiness" of printed material sending readers online and online readers being driven back to print—will be crucial in developing your future social media campaigns.

Measurement at the Speed of a Mouse

One of the reasons traditional marketing is becoming less effective is that industrial marketers are finding online campaigns and social media interactions easier to track. The effectiveness of print advertising, trade shows, and other traditional means of marketing your products is further hampered by a decided lack of means of measurement.

Online metrics, such as website traffic that can be narrowed down into lead conversions, which can be narrowed down to new customers, gives marketers the power to allocate marketing dollars to areas that are generating revenue more accurately than ever before.

While it might take months to determine whether appearing in a particular trade journal was effective, you can know immediately how many visitors, leads, prospects, and customers a recent campaign is generating; if it's not comparable to previous efforts, you can switch gears or change tactics within days or hours. This gives companies a new form of adaptability, which is becoming crucial for remaining relevant in today's market.

This immediacy of reporting is allowing those who take advantage of the industrial marketing revolution to pull ahead of their more traditional counterparts by making faster, better informed marketing and promotional decisions.

The Mass Marketing Migration

If there's one big lesson for marketers in this recent turn of events, it's that the old forms of marketing have been underperforming for quite some time now and should not be tolerated as the primary part of your all-important media mix.

To stay loyal to a trade journal or direct mailing company because you've been doing business with them for decades is charity, not capitalism. If an advertising stream has dried up, don't keep going back to the same well; instead, try to find a new (revenue) stream!

As a marketer, you must be prepared to think differently about your approaches to connecting with customers, prospects, and markets. Even before our recent economic problems hit, marketing was steadily trending away from traditional media, such as printed trade journals and in-person trade shows, and toward interactive web media, such as online search, e-newsletters, virtual events, and banner advertising. Today, content-based assets are critical elements to any successful marketing campaign. Throw in social media, and we're in the midst of a true revolution.

This "mass marketing migration" is steady, ongoing, and nearly complete, and it is always evolving and becoming more powerful. Your target audience has already begun migrating online to find you; as social media grows and traditional media continues to struggle, they are in no hurry to leave.

But more than *where* they are, we need to understand *why* they are there. Here are a few statistics that demonstrate how the behavior of your customers and prospects has changed:

- More than 80 percent of engineering, technical, manufacturing, and industrial professionals use the Internet to find components, equipment, services, suppliers, and product specifications. And 73 percent spend three or more hours per week on the Internet for work-related purposes. Your audience is online; you need to be there to connect with them.

- Four of the top five resources that technical professionals use when searching for products, services, and suppliers are online resources: general search engines, online catalogs, supplier websites, and online directories. The only non-online source to make the top five is "peers/ colleagues."
- Engineers and other technical professionals prefer web-based content to printed trade magazines as an information source. Over the past twelve months, 30 percent have reduced the use of printed trade magazines, continuing a documented trend over the past several years. However, 56 percent receive three or more e-newsletters, and 46 percent read e-newsletters at least daily or several times a week.

If It's Not Marketing as Usual, What Are Suppliers Doing?

Few, if any, experts expect the old ways of marketing and advertising to ever truly recover in the wake of "new" media. Even advertising agencies see the writing on the wall.

According to *AdWeek*, "Experts say agencies will not be able to simply return to business as usual. Some will be better positioned to grab a greater share of spending than others, say industry watchers, and those with the edge will be the ones that can optimize the use of digital media."

The article goes on to point out that most "new media" marketers will "rely on a portfolio of marketing and media vehicles, allowing them to reach with greater precision and greater accountability than they ever had before."

On the supplier side, many manufacturers have already adopted the new reality of online, social, and interactive marketing. According to the recent survey, "Trends in Industrial Marketing," 30 percent of industrial marketers are reducing trade show attendance—and 38 percent are reducing print ads. What is taking the place of these traditional media? For 48 percent, online marketing has become a greater portion of the marketing budget.

In addition, three of the top four sources of leads for manufacturers in are online programs: company websites, online sourcing directories and search engines, and e-mail marketing.

Measurement and Accountability Are Here to Stay

With the steadily dwindling ROI of traditional media, the measurement of marketing effectiveness is fast becoming a priority across all industries, but particularly in manufacturing and production. It continues to command increased attention as executives demand accountability from marketing, and measurement will remain a mandate as online numbers swell and marketing is the beneficiary of more investment, not less.

Manufacturers recognize the need for marketing measurement; in a recent survey, they strongly agreed with this statement: "There is greater pressure to demonstrate accountability and return on marketing investments."

Like most companies, manufacturers resist investing marketing dollars without knowing what they are getting for their return, but the effectiveness of print ads, trade shows, and other forms of traditional marketing have always been difficult to measure.

Now more than ever, manufacturers are closely evaluating the performance of marketing programs, reducing or eliminating those that don't perform well, and choosing marketing programs that are measurable.

In response to these changing times, 69 percent of manufacturers will closely evaluate the performance of marketing programs and reduce or eliminate programs that don't perform well, and 53 percent will choose marketing programs that are measurable.

The demand for measurement is also infiltrating the world of advertising agencies as clients have come to expect more accountability. Agencies will need a good understanding of measurable programs, know which ones will work for specific client objectives, and be able to deploy them for their clients.

Measurability Matters

Online marketing has proven to be extremely effective, and it is equally measurable. Online campaigns are built around impressions, clicks, and conversions—metrics that can effectively be captured and analyzed.

Take virtual events, for example. These online trade shows (which we'll discuss at length in later chapters) can track every move registered attendees make from the time they enter the digital door: which vendors they visit, time spent, materials downloaded, discussions, and more.

Imagine the benefits of such immediate, measurable data. Leads can be scored and prioritized according to online behavior, helping an exhibiting company plan its response and convert more leads to customers. Compare that to a fishbowl of random business cards or scanned ID badges collected at a trade show or the skewed responses in a customer questionnaire.

The ability to track the number of visitors to a web page tailored for a specific event or product, the number of clicks on an accommodating online ad, and the number of visitors converted to leads for any online offer creates a new streamlined sales cycle that promotes more customer conversions in shorter periods of time.

As we delve more deeply into content marketing, such measurable data becomes even more valuable. We can track which kind of content is most valuable to readers, how they—and how many—respond to particular keywords, topics, programs, and incentives. We begin to have the ability to put revenue-based value on specific keywords, e-mail campaigns, and more.

The key takeaway for marketers is to *make sure you have tools to measure their effectiveness and measure the things that matter* in any marketing programs you choose. This will allow you to see what works and what doesn't—and will justify your marketing investments while offering sales a more effective pipeline.

Online Marketing: *Beyond the Basics*

By now, it should be almost painfully clear how, and why, your customers and prospects have long since migrated to the Internet to search out and locate products, services, and suppliers.

You probably have an Internet presence as well. But at this point in the maturation of the Internet and its place in the business world, you need more—in many cases much more—than a company website to be effective online. You can't just drive anonymous clicks to your website. It's no longer Online Marketing 101, which previously promoted simply being there.

To gain visibility into key markets, attract the attention of customers and prospects, and generate qualified leads that translate into legitimate sales opportunities, today's successful industrial companies must deploy a portfolio of integrated, online programs that work together to achieve marketing and sales objectives.

Consider these examples of effective online marketing programs:

- Targeted e-newsletters and content delivered to specific industrial audiences based on individual online behavior. Prospects click on your offer, such as a white paper or webinar, and are directed to landing pages with conversion forms that generate leads. They are then sent individualized follow-up literature, automatically, based on their interests and needs to streamline the process through your defined sales cycle. This is completed before wasting a salesperson's time.
- Searchable online catalogs of parts and components that deliver leads with full contact information and areas of prospect interest help expedite an appropriate response and increase sales opportunities. Each product is optimized to show up in search engines, expanding your target market to people in need, who have not yet been identified.

13

- Robust listings in online searches allow an industrial audience to find your company description, technical articles, products, services, and more.
- Retargeting ads dispersed over targeted industrial websites increases the visibility of your company and invites prospects to click-through and take advantage of offers after they have shown interest in your products—but have not yet converted.
- Host industry-specific online trade shows where you can chat and interact with prospects, and showcase your products and services; in the end, you will have a list of every prospect who interacted with you and to what degree.

There are common threads running through all of these online marketing programs: they are targeted to a specific industrial audience, they are aimed at streamlining the conversion and qualification processes, and their performance is measurable—exactly what you need to put in place to be ready for the economic recovery.

Survey Says, "Technology Is the Future"

During the first quarter of 2011, GlobalSpec conducted its annual Industrial Marketing Trends Survey of marketing and sales professionals in the manufacturing sector. The survey addressed the marketing trends, challenges, and expenditures within the engineering, technical, manufacturing, and industrial communities.

Of the 384 survey respondents, 78 percent hold management positions in sales or marketing, and 10 percent indicate they are a president/CEO. This group represents a variety of company sizes; annual marketing budgets range from under $50,000 to over $1 million.

Highlights of the survey responses include:

- 87 percent of companies anticipate an increase in sales compared to 2010, a strong indicator of a better industrial economy.

- For the second year in a row, marketing budgets are recovering after a down year in 2009; 38 percent are spending more in 2011 than in 2010.
- 71 percent stated that customer acquisition or lead generation is their primary marketing goal in 2011. These have been the top two marketing goals for the past three years.
- The top three marketing challenges in 2011 are not enough quality leads, having too few resources, and the need to drive more customers to the company's website.
- 50 percent of companies are allocating more of their marketing budget to online programs in 2011, and 49 percent of companies spend more than a third of their marketing budget online.
- Three out of four sources for leads are online marketing channels; company websites are the number-one source of leads.
- The top three channels where industrial companies will increase spending in 2011 are video, social media, and search engine optimization (SEO).
- For the first time, the majority of companies (57 percent) plan to use social media applications in 2011.
- The most-used social media applications are LinkedIn (69 percent), Facebook (53 percent), and Twitter (44 percent).

As sales for manufacturers increase, so does their marketing spending; 87 percent of companies expected sales to increase in 2011 over 2010 levels. This is the second year in a row where a strong majority of companies anticipated increased sales.

Another sign the economy is on the upswing is that marketing expenditures are going up; 38 percent of industrial companies are increasing marketing. This growth is 7 percent higher than the previous year—and a healthy 22 percent higher than the economic lows of 2009.

Manufacturers face the same marketing challenges and goals every year. For the second consecutive year, *not generating enough high quality leads for sales* tops the list of manufacturers' biggest marketing problems (52 percent selected this as one of their top three problems). Rounding out the top three were *too few resources for marketing* and *the need to drive more customers to their website.*

At the same time, customer acquisition and lead generation remain the top two marketing goals for the fifth year in a row; 19 percent of companies reported brand awareness as their primary marketing goal, up from 13 percent since 2010, indicating the increasing importance of being noticed and recognized in crowded, competitive markets.

Emerging marketing channels are taking hold in the industrial sector. As a vibrant indicator of the mushrooming effect of forming strong online relationships to increase sales, significantly more companies (57 percent) are using social media as a marketing channel in 2011 than in 2010 (24 percent).

LinkedIn, Facebook, Twitter, videos, and blogs are all seeing increased usage in 2011 over 2010; LinkedIn, the most popular social media application, is used by 69 percent of companies. Also, 63 percent of companies are increasing spending in social media, 64 percent of companies are increasing spending in video, and 47 percent of companies are spending more on online events. One common thread of these emerging marketing channels: *they are all online.*

Online marketing is manufacturers' number-one area of marketing investment. The top eight channels for increased marketing spending in 2011 are all online—from social media and SEO to retargeted advertising networks, online newsletter sponsorships, and more.

In addition, companies spend an average of 38 percent of their marketing budget online, and 50 percent report that online marketing is a bigger percentage of their overall marketing budget than in previous years.

Although industrial companies are increasing their online marketing investments, they should do more because the industrial audience has largely migrated online to search for products, suppliers, and services. Online marketing programs can precisely target this audience—with measurable results.

Where Do You Allocate Marketing Dollars?

In the industrial sector, the percentage of marketing dollars invested in various media channels has been shifting significantly over the past few years. As engineering, technical, industrial, and manufacturing professionals turn to the Internet first to find product and service information, it's no surprise that a greater percentage of marketing program dollars are being shifted to online marketing.

Online resources have replaced printed directories and trade magazines as the top information resources for your audience. This makes it easier for you to find new customers; you already know where to reach them—on the Internet.

Are you reallocating dollars to more effectively reach your target audience of engineering, technical, industrial, and manufacturing professionals? Use the worksheet below to input the dollar amount and percentage of your marketing budget you spend on each media channel. Compare previous year expenditures to planned expenditures.

Seven Steps for Successfully Navigating Your Marketing Plan

Few things are as frustrating as mounting an industrial marketing campaign only to watch it crash and burn—except for watching it die a slow, miserable online death. The time, energy, resources, and money spent on such an endeavor makes the misfire all the more costly for all involved.

One way to discourage failure and ensure success is to think long and hard about how to succeed before mounting a campaign, not about what went wrong after. The following seven steps are designed to help you do just that:

Step 1: *See the finish line first.*

Every successful industrial marketing campaign begins with a clear goal in sight—a "finish line" mapped out well before pulling up to the starting gate.

Be specific about your goals; know what you want to achieve before assembling a team or setting guidelines, parameters, deliverables, and deadlines. Build time for careful planning into any marketing schedule to avoid costly mistakes once it begins.

Step 2: *Keep your hands on the steering wheel.*

At the rate technology is evolving today, oftentimes gadgets, gizmos, websites, and metrics that weren't available when you started a marketing campaign are par for the course by the time you finish. Trends change, and not every social media site is appropriate for every campaign.

Sometimes the only constant is change. Objectives shift to align with business goals, new marketing channels enter the mix, and prospects begin using different resources to obtain relevant business information. Therefore, unless you've proven your current program is optimized for today's marketing environment, your plan needs to evolve accordingly.

Evaluate your course often—and change direction as it becomes necessary. While no campaign should be built on a foundation of uncertainty or whimsy, don't be so rigid in your deadlines and deliverables that you can't be open to change along the way.

Step 3: *Stay in the right lane.*

Know where your target audience lives—and stay in the same lane with them. Do you know where your target audience spends the bulk of their time? Can you reach them there, comfortably and creatively, within the guardrails of your current industrial marketing campaign?

Virtually all engineering, technical, and industrial professionals use the Internet throughout their work processes. Are you reaching this target audience where they can be found looking for products and services like yours? Or are you still tossing your line into the ponds of traditional media, which are rapidly drying up?

Step 4: *Keep hitting your target.*

Many industrial marketers believe that knowing their target audience is enough, or that creating a unique message for each battle of the campaign—Facebook, Twitter, online trade shows, websites, blogs, white papers, and e-books—is enough.

Equally as important as finding your target audience and writing directly to them is *how often you are reaching them.* Are you pushing your message out to the market on a regular basis—or are your efforts sporadic at best? Are you attracting engineering, technical, and industrial professionals while they are looking and where they are looking for the products and services you have to offer?

Step 5: *Understand that less miles = more mileage.*

Avoid the "more is more" mentality that so many industrial marketers take. They are only "grabbing numbers" and "adding friends" as if quantity matters more than quality.

Instead, focus on refining your message(s) and making unique, valuable, and personal connections. Leads that provide intelligence to begin a relationship and gain a customer are more valuable than piles of nameless, faceless clicks. Be sure to capture relevant information.

Step 6: *Take the carpool lane.*

Oftentimes we create, conceptualize, and even complete an industrial marketing campaign in a bubble. We meet our needs—creatively, goal-wise, deliverable-wise—but we fail to check in with the sales team or anyone else who will directly benefit from the work we're doing.

At the beginning of the campaign, not the end, be sure to align yourself with anyone your marketing efforts will touch to make sure that all your needs are being met.

Step 7: *Follow the speed limit.*

Every successful industrial marketing campaign I've ever been involved in has had a pace, a rhythm, and its very own "speed limit." Don't get me wrong; every campaign should have guardrails, limits, deadlines, and deliverables, but be sure to build "time" in ahead of time.

If there is one truism to marketing, it's that *customers have their own timetables.* Contests, promotions, expiration dates, freebies, giveaways, guest posts, interviews, grand openings, and other "limited-time offers" need to be run with the understanding that it may take several impressions for a prospect to act, a lead to close, or an opportunity to present itself. When the time for such impressions is built into the original marketing plan, expectations can be adjusted and new definitions of success understood.

Five Don'ts to Avoid Before Starting Your Industrial Marketing Campaign

We've already seen what paths you should take before starting your industrial marketing campaign—why don't we check out five don'ts to avoid before you get started:

The First Don't: *Don't use a template.*

Successful marketing is original—for each market, each segment, each audience, each time. Certainly various tips, tactics, strategies, and algorithms can and should be repeated and applied across a variety of formats, but the content—and never forget that, with industrial marketing or any marketing, content is king—should always be original.

Don't repeat the same tweet day after day—same words, same time—for the same result. Alternate the times you tweet, comparing midmorning versus midafternoon. Write a new message, compare shorter versus longer tweets, etc.

Don't tweet exclusively; alternate between tweeting and exploring Facebook. Post on your blog and then upload a new video clip to YouTube. Repeat when you can—but never recycle old content in favor of new.

The Second Don't: *Don't neglect new markets.*

Where is your target audience gathering? Online trade shows? LinkedIn? Twitter? Facebook? Is there a new technology, website, or popular forum gaining momentum that you should know about?

Start—and end—every marketing day with these questions. Stay alert for new markets and new avenues to reach those markets. Learn how to use those markets.

While stale, static, and template-driven marketing plans are easier, vibrant, creative, and original industrial marketing campaigns that allow for variety, ingenuity, and the ability to turn on a dime to chase a new market will ultimately deliver more ROI.

The Third Don't: *Don't let dust gather on your marketing materials.*

Just as you must remain alert for new markets to open up during a campaign, it is important to stay current, fresh, and relevant with your marketing materials as well.

Ask yourself, objectively and with a fresh pair of eyes:

- Would this cause me to act?
- Does the description on the website include the latest specs/pictures for this product?

- Would this make me click to read more?
- Could our graphics benefit from a redesign?
- Does this message/language help build our brand?

If you can't answer yes to a question, rework the material until you can!

The Fourth Don't: *Don't ignore new media partners.*

Preparing targeted, online marketing programs may be new to you, but you shouldn't have to do it alone. This is a good time to consult with an experienced online media partner that understands and has the attention of the industrial audience you need to reach.

Discuss your marketing objectives and have them show you an integrated marketing program that will help you achieve your objectives and provide measurement and accountability.

The Fifth Don't: *Don't forget to measure.*

Measure, measure, and then measure some more. The beauty of online marketing campaigns is that they are easily measured, often in "real time." Today, the most effective marketing programs are online programs whose performance can be measured and analyzed. Online programs are built around impressions, clicks, and conversions.

You can easily see what is working and focus marketing dollars on the most successful programs, which will help reduce waste while increasing results.

Parting Words about the Death of Traditional Marketing

I am not suggesting that you do away with what works about your traditional marketing—that's what a proper "media mix" is all about. I am merely providing facts, figures, and commentary about the current state of traditional marketing and how global shifts in its effectiveness and timing are leading to a massive marketing migration online.

By noting the trend, and actively responding to it, you can gradually—or even not so gradually—transition from the traditional to the modern by taking advantage of the new media trends we'll be discussing in later chapters.

CHAPTER 2

The 365-Day Trade Show—The Power of Your Website

Some might consider their website a sign, even a symptom, of the death of traditional marketing. Websites were once the flavor of the day. Like a Facebook page, Twitter profile, or LinkedIn account, everyone had to get one or feel left out.

Unfortunately, many companies "threw up" a website, added a few links and some product descriptions—and called it a day. These sites were rarely any more interactive than a good postcard mailer, billboard, or print ad. It was "traditional marketing" because they didn't take advantage of the online medium any more than a generic e-mail blast about a new product or price drop.

Charles Dickens wrote, "It was the best of times, it was the worst of times." To take advantage of today's massive online marketing power via our websites and Internet promotions, we need to spend a few minutes turning back the dial to say how much, and how little, online marketing has changed since Web 1.0.

Websites: The Permanent Shift from "Me" Marketing to "We" Marketing

It's not just technology that's changed the power of modern websites; the attitude, the needs, and the empowerment of the end user have undergone a true revolution.

In the infancy of web-based marketing (or Web 1.0 as we call it now), all anyone did—even the era's top online promoters—was throw up a website and shout, "Look at me. Look at what great products I have. And now you can order/buy them online!"

It was a technological revolution first—and a marketing revolution second. The idea of ordering products online, or even looking at them online, was so revolutionary that none of us had time to consider the consumer experience other than to say, "They love it!

And they did . . . for a while. But static images on a never-changing website could only be novel for so long. Where early companies were quickly first to market with a new website and plenty of links, once the rest of the world caught up, what was left to do to compete?

As the web evolved, as new websites flooded the market and the novelty soon wore off, bells and whistles, shopping carts, and "zoom in/zoom out" features were no longer cutting edge. Customers wanted more from their websites; they wanted interactivity, inclusion, and engagement.

What could they click on? Were there "online only" specials? Where could they leave a comment? A review? A gripe or a kudo? Could they learn about the CEO? Follow his or her blog? Contact him or her personally?

The quick and demanding presence of so many online customers both pleased and frustrated many companies. When it was still just Web 1.0, companies felt that websites were a necessary evil, the cost of doing business in the modern marketplace. Back then, a presence was enough; it was all that was demanded or expected of them.

As a result, many companies put up quick websites and left it at that. They were little more than electronic billboards or online brochures; click a few links, turn a few pages—and you're done.

When social media arrived and brought with it the current version of the web, or Web 2.0, it was no longer enough to have a few pages outlining your company or your products.

Suddenly—quite suddenly for most—it became necessary to engage your customers and determine specific points of the sales cycle that your website would tailor to.

Visitors stopped being content with merely a website; they wanted an experience. They wanted a completely interactive and involving experience that wasn't just a one-off thing. They wanted an invitation to come back, engage, then engage some more. End users began craving engagement on the web. They wanted to be noticed and be assisted in ways that were *personal* and *particular* to their individualized needs.

And they wanted a different experience each time. Facebook, Twitter, Tumblr, LinkedIn, Goodreads, every new Web 2.0 website increased this high-level, high-intensity demand for content, growth, interactivity, experience, and engagement.

We're currently in a stage where consumers and businesses expect to be engaged and expect to easily have their needs accommodated via the web. Web 2.0 is more than just another gimmicky business term or phrase coined to sell more books, white papers, and magazine articles. It's a revolution within a revolution—a battle cry for those who would heed its call: "Lead, follow, or get out of the way!"

Arm Yourself with the Power of Your Industrial Marketing Website

The message of Web 1.0 versus 2.0 is clear: just because something is online doesn't necessarily make it *online marketing*—and just marketing online doesn't make it *effective online marketing*. We, as an industry, need to start seeing our websites less as billboards or

3-D print ads (i.e. Web 1.0) and more of an interactive, always open, twenty-four-hour-a-day online trade show (i.e. Web 2.0). What does a trade show offer besides exposure, hands-on sampling of product, personal interaction with sales reps and staffs, and an intense, one-on-one introduction to a company, idea, or brand?

Your website, when done right, can do all those things and more:

- **Exposure**: An attractive, easy-to-navigate website is your frontline, first assault on a viewer's senses. It is instant and, ideally, positive exposure to all your company does—from personnel to product, from philosophy to processing. Every graphic, every word, all content and features should be focused to make this first exposure a lasting and positive impact that will eventually translate to sales.
- **Hands-on sampling of product**: Okay, so maybe "hands on" is a stretch, but with today's graphics, zoom-in and pull-out features, and great photos and specs of each of your products, online visitors can have as close to one-on-one interactivity with your product as if they were actually there in person, picking up each item and physically manipulating them by hand.
- **Personal interaction with sales reps and staff**: With the right features, support staff, a preexisting Q&A, and other bells and whistles, your website can act as a virtual meeting place for customers and sales reps/staff to interact in a real, genuine manner.
- **One-on-one introduction to a company, idea, or brand**: A cohesive, branded website that is carefully thought out can send a clear, strong message about who you are, what you sell, and what you stand for—in customer service, expertise, established credentials and credibility, and even the company's personal and professional corporate vision.

The good news about this second industrial (marketing) revolution is that you already have the most powerful weapon around: *your website*. While they may not seem as sexy as other forms of marketing—social media has been hogging most of the spotlight lately—never forget that all social media drives traffic. You decide where that traffic goes—and it should all lead *right back to your website.*

Warning: this is not a technical chapter on how to build a website! It is a motivational chapter about why your website is so important—and how you can make it even more important to your customers. First, let's find out a few things your website *is* and *isn't.*

Ten Things Your Website Is

1.) A living, breathing online presence
2.) A branding tool
3.) A "convenience store" for today's 24/7 shopping culture
4.) An online catalog that is fully interactive
5.) A cornucopia of content for online users to devour
6.) A hub for all your industrial marketing efforts
7.) A constantly updated, frequently tweaked expression of your corporate self
8.) A powerful ally in your own industrial marketing revolution!
9.) An important, and open, conduit between you and the consumer
10.) A twenty-four-hour trade show for your company, your expertise, your products, and your personnel

Ten Things Your Website Isn't

1.) A billboard
2.) A print ad
3.) A screensaver
4.) A bumper sticker
5.) A brochure
6.) A business card
7.) A chore

8.) An excuse

9.) A postcard

10.)A "build-it-and-forget-it" exercise

Five Secrets of a Powerful Website

Now more than ever, industrial marketers rely on a website to supercharge online promotional efforts. As you can see from the above exchange, there are as many things your website *is* as what it *isn't*, and it's important to make those distinctions before moving forward.

In industrial marketing, it is easy to keep the status quo, particularly when it comes to technical aspects of your promotional efforts like a website. From design to content to linkages and graphics, the prevailing sentiment among most industrial marketers seems to be, "If it ain't broke, why fix it?"

But you'll never know just what's broken, and how badly, if you never take a closer look at your website—how it works, why it works, how it doesn't, and *why* it doesn't.

Many books, courses, webinars, seminars, and courses explain how to design a website; far be it for this section to try to improve on those. However, here are some simple, commonsense, no-muss-no-fuss tips you might not have read in those other books:

1. **The hub effect:** Treating your website like a static, unchanging billboard, bumper sticker, or business card detracts from its usefulness. Instead, look at it as the hub of your online activity. Every linkage, promotional opportunity, and collateral marketing piece you send should share one link—your website link—as the hub where every user is directed. Even if you have a lot going on on your website, such as a free e-book, a blog, or an online catalog, those should all be found easily on your main website to avoid confusion or diffusion of your central message.

2. **Expect to change:** As happy as you may be with your website today, expect it to change tomorrow, the next day,

and beyond. Every new product description, every new line, and every new client testimonial, award, policy, or personnel change deserves an update.

3. **Click a mile in your user's mouse:** Don't assume that your users have or will spend the time to hunt down the various features, promotions, offers, and product descriptions on your website. View your website objectively and click a mile in your user's mouse; see how it feels from the user's perspective. Notice the times, clicks, links, or experiences where you experience frustration.

4. **Less is more:** Take time and get feedback to ensure that your web layout is as simple, straightforward, focused, and streamlined as possible. Even when you're using it as a hub for all your online activity, there are still ways to make it streamlined and accessible—and a pleasant viewing experience—for all online visitors.

5. **Lead with the headline:** What is the most important message you want to share with online visitors? What is the second-most important message? Third, fourth, and fifth? Just as Kellogg's, Nabisco, Gatorade, Coke, and Pepsi fight for the coveted "eye-level aisle" on the grocery shelves, consider your eye level to ensure that what visitors want most—as opposed to what sales, marketing, or even the CEO want most—is prominent, clearly visible, and fully usable. Maybe that "Letter from the CEO" doesn't need such a prominent place on the website when 92 percent of visitors click first on the interactive catalog, new products, or current deals link.

Starting Where You Are, Going Where You're Meant to Be

The beauty of your website is that it already exists; the challenge is turning it into an industrial marketing masterpiece via a perhaps revolutionary site design (see next section)! That can take time, energy, expertise, and even expert help. Regardless, you'll never know where you want to go if you don't stop and take a look at where you are.

Ask yourself some simple questions to about your current website before you begin to reimagine, plan, and redesign it:

- Are you happy with it in its current state?
  - o If so, why are you happy?
  - o If not, why are you unhappy?
- What do readers think?
- Is there even a comment or contact us button for them to tell you what they think?
- How interactive is it?
- How interactive could it be?
- Have any focus groups weighed in on the subject?
- Are you open to constructive criticism?
  - o If so, how open?
  - o If not, why not?
- Have you gotten any constructive criticism?

The answers to these and other questions will likely determine the destiny and direction of your website. For best results, ask them—and answer them—objectively.

The Salesperson Who Never Sleeps: A Few Words about the Importance of Your Website Redesign

If you're still reading this—if you picked up this book in the first place—you probably need a website redesign. Even if you think you don't, think again.

The power of your website cannot be underestimated; it is your most powerful marketing tool. In the hub mentality, your website is the center of your marketing universe; as such, it can't just "exist." It must exist with purpose.

When attempting a website redesign, it is important to follow the "less is more" philosophy. Many companies equate website redesign with more links, more pages, more text, and more pictures for more results. But we can't confuse clutter with control. Again, think of the end users. What will their experiences be like? How easily can they navigate it? Are their needs being met?

Your website isn't just an electronic billboard or hub for online busywork; it's the easiest way for a consumer to navigate through to a sale. It's a receptacle, a reservoir, and an active, living, breathing engine for lead generation.

A simple, effective, attractive, focused, interactive site design allows your company to streamline its sales cycle and automatically become *a salesperson that never sleeps.* To that end, it is the most valuable marketing tool a company can have.

Goals, Not Graphics: Seven Tips for an Effective Website Redesign

Like everything else in this industrial marketing revolution, we must consider a site redesign for the right reasons, not merely for the cosmetic, convenient, or cost-effective ones. In short, what is your primary goal for a redesign? Why are you doing it? How will it help? Who will it help? What will visitors think of it?

Seven Tips for an Effective Website Redesign

1.) **Less is more:** Keep it simple, focused, and easy to navigate. When meetings get intense and consultants get excited and designs are kicked around and suggested, never forget to ask, "What will the end user experience be like? Can they quickly find the pages, portals, and content that will contribute to leads and lead to sales?

2.) **Metrics, measurement, and meaning:** No matter who is doing your redesign, make sure they are making it easy, simple, and quick to measure the performance and profitability of each website component.

3.) **Content is king:** Rather than focus on the bells and whistles of a completely original, unique, and explosive web design, focus your manpower, muscle, and budget on creating quality content that is engaging, powerful, unique, and inviting.

4.) **Content is constant:** Plan, prepare and hire for constant content updating. If your blog and social media presence are integral to your own online industrial marketing revolution, you can't just fill your "home," "about us" and "contact us" pages and leave it at that. Plan for content to be continually refreshed and schedule, or even hire, accordingly.

5.) **Don't fix what's not broken:** If something currently works on your website, don't fix it—leave it alone! An expensive, time-consuming website do-over can actually hurt more than it helps if you throw out the baby with the bathwater by removing, eliminating, or forgetting the original design or content elements that worked fine.

6.) **Do it for the right reasons:** Your goals are generating more leads, forming stronger consumer alliances, and increasing sales; these are the right goals for a website redesign. Unfortunately, companies often redesign a website because it's been a year or more since the last redesign!

7.) **Blogging for fun and profit:** A blog should be part of any modern industrial marketing revolution website redesign. It is important to have the element where content is king and constantly updated to provide the engagement, education, information, and interactivity that Web 2.0 visitors demand.

Parting Words about Your Wonderful Website

Any website is a good website. But is good really good enough? In today's competitive marketplace, good is often the starting line—and "best" dashes across the finish line first.

You are only as good as your last click. As your website grows, expands, shrinks, tightens, and generally evolves, customers will forget what it looked like yesterday in favor of how it looks today. For better or worse, what you do with your website from this point on is all anyone will ever remember. Make those changes count!

CHAPTER **3**

Your Biggest Competitive Advantage

The Internet hasn't just revolutionized industrial marketing; it has become your biggest competitive advantage.

Imagine a field where all the normal rules of strength, speed, agility, and competitive advantage apply. Bigger means stronger, faster means better, more expensive uniforms and training allow for untold gains as you and your company stand, clutching your helmets and trembling, on the other side of the field.

Now imagine the same scenario: you and your small business team are about to go up against the Dells, the Microsofts, and the Apples of the competitive world with their superior muscle, speed, organizational agility, and nearly unlimited spending power and, poof, right before the kickoff, someone turns off the gravity!

Suddenly, all bets are off. Strong players, weak players, fast players, great uniforms, awesome helmets—none of it matters. You're all starting at square one—with zero gravity. No one knows how to run, let alone jump, pass, block, or tackle because no one has experienced anything like this before. Suddenly, the odds are even—and you're all on a level playing field.

Welcome to the Internet. I like to call it the second (Marketing) Industrial Revolution. The web has transformed your company's ability to compete in competitive markets and reach target markets with the same efficiency as corporate spenders who previously bought their way to the top.

The Cost of Doing Business, Then and Now

This section is about how technology, specifically the web, has changed the competitive landscape of industrial marketing—really, of *all* marketing—forever.

Before the web became standard operating procedure for marketing departments worldwide, advertising was all about *spending more* to *gain more*. Large corporations, such as Procter &Gamble, McDonald's, and Pepsi, spent more than their competition to reach a greater audience, resulting in a greater market share. More placements, more television, more radio—it all came down to buying more.

What could a small, start-up soda company do to out-promote Coca-Cola? How could a small mom and pop hardware store compete with Ace, True Value or Wal-Mart? They couldn't. Like some medieval caste system, small companies were expected to stay small while the Fortune 100 took the lion's share of profit.

The competitive landscape was defined, and dominated, by one simple variable: who had the most money to spend? Some of this brick-and-mortar mentality is still present today. Physical tradeshows, for instance, are still very much the same as they were in their infancy.

Who can spend the most money to create an existence at more trade shows, at more conferences, and the like? The folks in our industry who spend the most still have the biggest presence at trade shows and conferences; they "own" the space and feel comfortable there.

Then, as now, who can compete with them? It wasn't logical for a smaller company to be able to compete with large corporations because they didn't have the resources—financial or otherwise—to force their message in front of the same number of buyers.

The cost of traditional, old school media, including television, radio, billboards, direct mail, and other traditional means of advertising were not attainable on smaller budgets, leaving advertising to be controlled wholesale by corporate giants.

Content: Leveling the Playing Field

Today, that "David-versus-Goliath" mentality has changed greatly, thanks in large part to the web and the rise of "conversational" social media. Now the marketplace is created—and powered—by the buyer.

It is no longer a one-way "lecture" between print and traditional media advertising where readers look but don't touch, listen but don't talk, and see but don't participate. Now it is more of a conversation; buyers lead much of the talk about their needs, expectations, desires, experiences, satisfaction, or dissatisfaction.

The suddenly interactive nature of "the new web" means that the buyer has much more power in controlling how they buy and we, as an industry, have a much bigger stake in convincing that consumer to buy from us. The difference is that the playing field has gone from expensive delivery of content—billboards, ads, and commercials—to be stripped down to mostly just the content. Not just any content; it is the ability to create and match buyer needs to content.

Content is the driving force behind buying decisions; the expansive nature of technology and the Internet allows all companies to compete for the same audience and market share by producing content that is generated for the audience.

The ability to create content doesn't come with a price tag. All companies have the ability to compete in the massively growing electronic marketplace through search engines, social media, e-mail, and other forms of communication that are driven by buyers and not industry, which levels the playing field for all to compete. Buying power has shifted in a way that creates an abundance of marketplace opportunities. Buyers are obsessed with quickly accessing information from multiple sources for purchasing decisions. It's defining sources and targeting them to better inform buyers of your brand and products and become part of purchasing mix.

It doesn't take television, radio, or billboards to establish reach. Buyers are no longer interested in these advertising mediums; DVRs, satellite radio, and online banner advertising were created for the sole purpose of not interrupting a user's experience with unwanted ads. These additions allow them to control the content they are given.

It's Called the "Web" for Good Reason

The web creates a competitive advantage that was non-existent years ago. It allows companies to engage with the marketplace in a way that isn't measured in advertising dollars. The ability to deliver content is tailor-made for your target audience and streamlined to get them to buy from you.

You can own your little (for now) corner of the "web" and reach out, through content, words, images, descriptions, events, interaction, and dialogue to actively control the amount of contact you have with potential customers. You can, through trial and error, fine-tune your message and deliver better content and a better end-user experience to attract more customers and spread out, just like a real web, into untapped markets. You can spend more time focusing on the messages that matters most to your direct—or indirect—buyers instead of spending more money.

The web gives small and midsized companies the ability to carry out Fortune 100-style marketing strategies that wouldn't be possible in traditional media.

Why You Don't Have to Reinvent the Wheel

One of the most bittersweet revelations about the web is that it is completely transparent. It's just as easy for customers to complain about you as it is for them to rave about you—and it's all there, online, permanently.

This is an incentive to take pains to create valuable, thoughtful content as well as to handle customer complaints swiftly and vocally to squelch bad press. It's also an opportunity to take the hard work, efforts, and expense of your competitors' marketing strategies and mine them carefully for clues about what works, what doesn't, and why.

Through modern technology, companies have the unique position to allow corporate giants to spend money on the electronic marketplace through paid advertising and pay-per-click (PPC) ads, take that intelligence and implement it into full-blown marketing campaigns for their own businesses.

The web gives companies the ability to deploy successful campaigns drawn out by corporate giants. Imagine recreating the successful Domino's "hidden video" campaign of customers talking about their new pizza only to learn they're being watched without having to actually do the focus groups, studies, campaigning, and researching to reveal if it would be successful or not.

In addition to being a vast marketing tool, the web is a valuable educational tool, a virtual R&D Department—for *free*—right there in living color as it plays out every day.

Whether it's your competitor's coupon campaign or their CEO's blog posts or those of Pizza Hut, Pepsi, and Powerade, there is always a wealth of vital and valuable intelligence available at your disposal with the click of a mouse. Google AdWords and other pay-per-click advertising programs give companies intelligence to determine where customers are. Your company has the ability to determine what valuable keywords are driving sales for your competitors, what keywords are not worth going after, and what type of ad copy is converting them on the web. It's all right there in front of you; all you need to do is put the pieces together.

Parting Words about Your Biggest Competitive Advantage

To recap the main points covered in this section, here are five reasons the web—and the emerging technology that makes it so powerful—is your greatest competitive advantage:

1.) **The global marketplace is now a level playing field for all to compete.** Forget the big marketing budgets that gave Fortune 100 companies supremacy over the rest of us. With ingenuity, imagination, and inventiveness, you can compete—even surpass—the corporate giants through tailored, effective content.

2.) **Companies can take intelligence from every competitor in their field to sculpt targeted, efficient marketing campaigns.** Use the transparency of the web to your advantage by creating a "culture of creativity." Closely follow your competitors' campaigns that work to learn how, why, when, and how to replicate them on an appropriate scale for you and your customer base.

3.) **Companies can actually control market share through content instead of spending.** Forget the "spend more, make more" mentality that fueled traditional advertising for decades. Focus on creating content, which costs less and allows you more control (see below for more on this topic).

4.) **Content is king.** Content—words, images, interaction, campaigns, messages, reactions, and responses—is the fuel that drives this industrial marketing revolution. Mastering the art of creating such content will propel you and your company to new heights.

5.) **Mind(s), not money, matters.** The past greatest advantage enjoyed by only corporate giants is no longer relevant, opening up a huge window of opportunity for those who can think fast, create more, and seize opportunities by being open-minded and willing to change.

PART
2

Attracting an Industrial Crowd

CHAPTER 4

Creating a Killer Content Machine

Content; it's all about the machinery. Due to the nature of the industry we work in, we have a leg up on every other social media participant on the planet. Industrial companies know the value of a good machine.

Above all else, a good machine cranks out parts without interruption to help the end user accomplish a need or solve a problem. Do you need twenty-three thousand widgets by the end of the day? How about four hundred thousand shoelaces, screws, nuts, bolts, or trays? There's a machine for that. The machine takes the materials you put in—paper, cotton, metal, thread, rubber, plastic, whatever—and gives you an end result.

In theory, content marketing is exactly the same.

What Is Content?

First, let's talk for a few seconds about what content is. Your website? Filled with content. Content drives your blogs, your tweets, your Facebook status updates, and newsletter articles.

Here are the some forms content can take in the life of an industrial marketer:

- your resume/CV
- your website's "About Us" page

43

- your website's "Company History" page
- your website's every page
- white papers
- journal articles
- books/e-books
- blog posts
- articles
- letters to the editor/consumer
- tweets
- texts
- YouTube videos
- Radio interviews or podcasts
- coupon copy
- brochures
- business cards
- banner ads
- blurbs
- responses to online critics/comments
- sales scripts

As you can see, pretty much any combination of creative words—that's what we're really talking about here—can be considered content.

Sometimes they'll be your own words or those of your staff. Other times, they'll be someone else's words—guest posts, commentators, customer reviews—or a post, "like," or "share" for an online article from an industrial journal, trade show, or thought leader.

Content is creative. It can be written, verbal, video, audio, short and sweet, long and considered, or academic or casual, but it is always creative.

Five Things Content Is

1.) **Fresh**: "Fresh" content can be hard to define, but you'll know it when you see it. If something makes you sit up and take notice—a clever slogan or tagline or headline or subtitle or tweet—you'll know it. Continually strive to create content that is fresh, energetic, creative, and *engaging*.

2.) **Unique**: Never forget that the unwritten prefix of *all* content is "unique" content. When you see the word content, think unique. Not just unique in the oddball, singular, eccentric case—but unique to you. What about this content makes it yours? How do you own it? Does it have a particular style, humor, grace, musculature, or "tone" that has your company written all over it?

3.) **New**: The point of any machine is not just to use it once and then let it sit there, gathering dust. Machines are designed for constant, repeated, and almost daily use. Your "killer content machine" should be working every day—if not at full capacity, then at least in a developmental, creative, and brainstorming way. Women's magazines have to think about six to eight months in advance when planning "holiday/seasonal" issues. As you begin developing content for your website/blog redo, or launch, consider doing the same so that you always have a pipeline of fresh content at the ready.

4.) **Original**: While there are many templates, services, and "devices" you can use to help automate your content, which is fine, avoid using them to create it. Generic, random, template-driven, fill-in-the-blank content is almost worse than no content at all because viewers easily see through it and learn that your website is, in reality, little more than an electronic billboard.

5.) **User-driven**: Finally, make it about the reader, the end user, the purchaser, the consumer. What do they want to read about and why? What information do they want—and how can you give it to them? Content, originality, tone, words, videos, blogs, and books are intended to inform, engage, educate, and drive the reader/end user to make a purchase at some point.

Five Things Content Isn't

1.) **Derivative**: Have you ever noticed that all some people tweet or post on Facebook are quotes by other people? Oscar Wilde, Gandhi, Martha Stewart, Thomas Jefferson, Beyoncé—it doesn't matter who it is—they cut and paste quotes from other people and let them fly all day long. That is not content. While it's okay to post the occasional quote, mix it up. Or at least follow it up with why you're posting this particular quote. Explain what the quote means to you, or the speaker, or what's going on with the company that drove you to post it.

2.) **Recycled**: Don't just have a big "ramp up" on content, hiring freelancers to craft dozens of blog posts and tweets and videos and podcasts and then recycle them over and over and over again. Instead, create a "content machine" that continually produces fresh, new, original, and unique content on a regular basis.

3.) **Boring**: Not every piece of content has to be Shakespeare or Twain, but it should never be boring!

4.) **Uninspired**: I am not suggesting you take a second job creating content just for the fun of it! Remember that the main goal of industrial marketing is increasing the bottom line. That said, for content to work at all, it must be inspired. It must interest people, engage them, and drive them to visit your site more often—and look through its pages more intensely. Becoming a customer is what's really at stake here.

5.) **Generic**: If your content is so generic that it looks like every other industrial website on the planet, why should users bother coming back to yours?

Content: It All Starts in Development

Most people create things with their own needs in mind. What do I want to say? How do I want to say it? The goal of developing content should be to begin understanding *the needs of your intended audience.*

- Who are they?
- What do they want to read/hear/see?
- What do they want to know?
- How much time do they have?
- What is important to *them*?

Content drives marketing in the traditional and online sense. People crave the information they seek, and there are a stunning variety of ways to get it. This information comes in a variety of ways, such as white papers, spec sheets, brochures, videos, people.

- It's all content.
- It's all information.
- It's all beneficial to the user.

Determining what your end users want—through trial and error if necessary—is the first step to developing what we all want in industrial marketing: *quality content that counts.*

Content makes the sales cycle go around. Each step of the sales cycle is met by a new inventory of content, defined specifically for that prospect's stage in learning why he or she should buy from you. Our next section will talk specifically about each of those "stages" and how they impact the end user.

The Four Types of Industrial Content

How readers read, and respond to, industrial marketing content is most effectively categorized into four main stages of awareness:

1.) **Discovery:** This first, initial phase of awareness starts when a prospect is seeking information on their needs. What, specifically, are their needs? This is the "awareness" stage where prospects discover a gap and begin to explore filling it. Having quality, continuous content and a strong web presence across a variety of marketing platforms—website, directories, SEO, social media, blogs, and white papers—sets the stage for those end users to discover you.

2.) **Research:** Once the need is identified, more specific information is determined for how they should go about the procurement process. Suppliers and their competitors are discovered and researched. This is the process where the buyer makes a mental note of "who has this available." The initial exposure to your website, brand, company, or content might be through a link, a topic search, or a recommendation.

3.) **Sourcing:** During the sourcing stage, a buyer becomes more actively engaged with companies to identify *who can best solve a particular problem*. During this stage, the buyer narrows down purchasing options by exploring product specs, adjusting requirements, and more. This stage requires guidance, and it is the first true interactive conversion where action is taken by the buyer. Here, content comes down to your online brand identity. What people know about you—online and elsewhere—is generally due to the content that's available. The more quality, individual, relevant content that speaks to your customers is available, the sooner you become the go-to source for their particular needs.

4.) **Procurement:** During this stage of the content cycle, buying decisions are made. This point of the process is when pricing is viewed, specifications are verified, and final questions are answered by various vendors. This is also typically where most companies stop their engagement and leave the customer in control of the process. It is the one true opportunity where companies can differentiate themselves through content aimed squarely at the end user.

Understanding the buying cycle and creating a machine of content to supply buyers with the resources they need for each stage of the cycle allows industrial manufacturers to identify clear needs and stay engaged with the buyer through each critical element of the sales cycle. Incidentally, this is called a "cycle" because content is driven by the customer—and the customer is driven by the content.

Parting Words about Your Killer Content Machine

This "cycle" is why content is so critical. It is the driving force behind the marketing and sales cycles while driving conversion in a uniformed way. The content machine must consistently be maintained, just as a traditional machine would be maintained.

The better the machine, the better the process.

CHAPTER 5

Content Strategy—Your New Inventory

Where industrial marketing used to be a "recycling bin" full of the same stock lines, phrases, blurbs, tag lines, ad copy, product descriptions, and brochure pages that were used over and over every year, today you must have an inventory of fresh, quality, unique, targeted content that drives brand loyalty and, ultimately, sales.

Much as you stock your warehouse shelves with plastics, parts, widgets, and fittings, you must make sure that your "content inventory" is also kept freshly stocked.

While this content may feel intangible or like another "soft skill" that's a luxury versus a necessity, it's not. In a very real way, in the very modern world of social media and technology (where everyone else is stocking their content inventory too), to run out of content affects your profits as much as running out of a product that you can touch, ship, and sell.

Stocking Your Content Shelves

To help maximize the content you create, you should vary it in forms, length, and where it might appear in the four main stages of awareness (more on those later in this chapter).

Here are some examples of "content inventory" you will need to stock your shelves:

- **White papers:** White papers are a valuable way to increase your expertise in a particular field or topic or with a specific audience with a relatively short, informative, and well-written piece. A 9-10 page white paper on a certain topic can help brand your company and provide the customer with information that none of your competitors is offering.

- **E-books:** Where white papers are fact-filled pieces in short form, e-books can be larger in scope and touch on a variety of larger issues and topics. For instance, while a white paper may touch on the topic of how to properly care for and maintain your company's door hinges, an e-book can broach broader issues—in longer form—such as the future of using different, longer-lasting, ecologically friendly materials in door hinges.

- **Articles:** Articles are a great way to associate your company with expertise. Having a professionally written article appear in a respected journal or website, particularly in a monthly or regular column, creates *the* impression that you are a company to take seriously and includes *multiple* impressions of your company, or CEO's, name.

- **Blog posts:** In three-hundred- to five-hundred-word "posts," your company can fill a blog with quality content designed specifically to educate and inform potential customers about your products, how to use them, care for them, store them, etc. Appearing often and in plainspoken language, blog posts can be a much more personal, almost casual one-on-one between a representative of your company and readers.

- **Social media posts:** Through constant and engaging social media interaction on websites, such as Facebook, Twitter, and YouTube, your industrial manufacturing company can create a wide and dependable presence that helps differentiate you from your competitors.

Consider each bullet point above a "shelf," and make sure to always keep it stocked with content. Write an e-book? Great. Now get another one in the pipeline so that you build up a "library" of reference material that potential customers can utilize, free of charge.

Write a white paper? Write two more. Number them in a series. Start a series. It's no different than stocking a shelf with door hinges, screws, nuts, bolts, or copper wire and thinking that it will still be there at the end of the week.

Getting yourself in the mindset of continually and constantly "restocking" your content inventory will gradually drive your awareness—and bottom line profits—up.

All Content Is Different; All Content's the Same

White papers. E-books. Articles. Blog posts. Tweets. Facebook messages. Letters to the editor. Video. All of it is content; all of it is uniquely different. A white paper, for instance, is shorter in length than an e-book and should stick to one particular topic, such as the strength of your new corrugated shipping boxes or the durability of your door hinges, in a way that is valuable for a customer. Your title may read, "Ten Ways to Save Money with Shipping Boxes."

This assures that, in true white paper fashion, a potential customer can find the white paper—usually through a Google search or link from an outside source—go to your site, see what you have to offer, download the white paper, and get the information he or she is looking for.

Meanwhile, an e-book could have broader and bigger implications, not just for readers but for your business. While you probably wouldn't want or need all of your white papers available on Amazon.com, having a professionally written, edited, and designed e-book available there could introduce you to thousands, maybe millions, of potential customers you might not have run across without it.

If you deal with a variety of safety issues in the production of your products, you might write an e-book entitled *Fifty-Two Tips for Job Safety in the Industrial Sector.* If you've written ten white papers, after the tenth individual release, combine them and you have a newly written e-book.

While this may not sound like a "customer magnet" for most people, for you it's a way to talk with expertise about a topic familiar to industrial manufacturers—and the clients who use your products.

It's Not about You

What all of this content is geared toward, regardless of its length or where people find it, is addressing the needs of your customers. It may not sound fun to write a book called *Fifty-Two Tips for Job Safety in the Industrial Sector,* but how many of your customers or potential customers or future customers might find that useful? A hundred? A thousand? A hundred thousand?

The goal of content creation is not only to be creative—but to get creative when it comes to industrial marketing. White papers, articles, e-books, and other types of useful, quality content make the industrial world go around. Every industrial company has information that can help potential customers in more ways than *just purchasing their product.*

The goal is to look deeper than yourself. Look past your needs, stop recycling content, and create something new, unique, and valuable—that your customers really want to read.

You need to assess the overall goal of your prospective customer and create content that will appeal to them. Whatever might interest, inform, engage, or enhance the life of your customer—safety, security, strength, variety, the future, or the past—ping those items as future ideas for creative content.

Don't Forget to Bring a Gift

Content is sharing. Sharing is expanding. Expanding is sexy. Sexy leads to content. That has pretty much been the theme for the past year in marketing. Content sharing has jumped to the forefront of the marketing mix and has taken over a large share of strategies around the web.

We are witnessing a marketing transition from what was once in-your-face or interruption-based marketing to a much more interactive and buyer-focused way to expanding brands to target audiences.

Over the past year, I've been blessed to represent and study some of the world's most influential industrial brands (although many do supply to the consumer-based world).

During a recent session, a client asked, "What truly is content sharing? It sounds like gifts." It was a good question. It was an even better point. In today's modern world of information, you can google "content sharing" and get a wide variety of prospective and insights.

The basic principle remains consistent—create pieces of content that are valuable to your audience and give it to them—but is that really all there is to it? Define what your audience determines is valuable and give it to them? No. Content needs to be carefully tailored with a purpose.

Many companies and marketers become consumed with the quantity of sharing—as opposed to the value of sharing. I completely understand, and promote, the benefits of growing your website and expanding your brand by creating content regularly—and sometimes that means turning content that would otherwise probably not be published.

That leaves an opportunity to optimize a new page of your website for search engines based on newly defined keywords, and that's great. But you must keep a core strategy in place when creating valuable content.

Content needs to be treated like gifts. Put thought into it and focus that thought on individual audiences, just as you would a birthday present for a good friend or a Christmas gift for a relative. To accomplish this, I recommend creating a list of what your audience is asking for. Answer these questions to get started:

- Who are you creating your content gift for?
- What do they need?
- What past discussions have you had with them about issues?
- What issues do they currently face?
- How can you solve these issues?
- What can you offer to solve these issues for free?

Once you've delved in a bit into your prospects needs, you can begin putting together your gift. I call content a gift because of the effect it has on people. Do you ever notice that you feel terrible when you receive a gift from someone and don't have one in return?

It's a sense of appreciation for receiving something—and then feeling obligated to return the favor. Odds are you won't forget that Christmas gift next year. The same concept applies to marketing and sales. Once you give someone something they find valuable, a sense of repayment is embedded subconsciously.

That's also why it's critical to create quality content around the customer's needs—not your own. Don't you have that one person on your list who gives you Christmas CDs every year, just because she likes to listen to Christmas CDs? It's not a gift if it's for yourself. Create content that your customers want to read—not necessarily that you want to write. (Although, ideally, the best written content is the kind you want to write *because* your customers will want to use it).

Once you've earned the trust of a prospect, the rest takes care of itself. People feel a debt to others who help them in their lives and in business. When the time comes that you have a solution that fits their problem, they kill two birds with one stone. Solve the problem—and repay a debt.

Creating a content gift list gives you the ability to strategically plan how you can become part of your potential customer's life without jumping in with a sales pitch. If there's anything we've learned from traditional marketing, it's that people do not like to be sold. Period. Don't interrupt your prospect's day with sales messages; become part of your prospect's day with resources.

Make Sure It Isn't Junk Mail

One of the more popular stalwarts of traditional media has been direct mail. Unfortunately, with rising postage prices and the immediacy of e-mail, social media, and technology, direct mail is fast becoming a thing of the past.

The problem is that many companies have relied on direct mail for so long—and they can't picture doing business without it. It's a little like the industrial marketer who sends out a million direct mail pieces and then goes home and complains about the junk in his mailbox!

Direct mail is physical and it's bulky. It shows up, unsolicited, and forces you to deal with it. Store it, file it, complain about it, or throw it out—whatever. Those reasons alone make it counterproductive. You never want to deliver content in a way that produces a negative reaction.

Electronic versions of content are less intrusive, more interactive, and more effective. You "opt in" to a company's newsletter. You click on a link. You read a tweet. Follow a Twitter account. Like a Facebook page. Follow a blog. Download a white paper or an e-book. In all these cases, the customer is driving the exchange.

When you create quality content, offer it in terms of a "gift," tailor it to your customer's needs, and make it voluntary, it's all forward motion. It's all momentum—and it's all up to them.

Design Your Content around the Four Types of Industrial Content

In the last chapter, I introduced you to the four main stages of awareness. In this section, I'd like to revisit each of those stages, paying particular attention to what kind of content you can create to make the particular stages even more compelling for you and your company.

The First Stage of Awareness: Discovery

Think of the vastness of the web, the abundance of online competition you face, the thousands and hundreds of thousands and millions of links there are for your customers to click on, and you get a feel for how daunting it can be for prospects to discover you. The days of throwing up a website and having customers stumble upon you are long over.

Today, it's about driving discovery. It's about funneling users to your site, your blog, your Facebook page, and your Twitter account. You do that with carefully designed content designed to entice, attract, and engage customers.

The more pieces of content you create to help customers discover you, the more you distinguish yourself from your competitors. This is where having a cleanly designed website comes in handy. Consider its layout. Can people quickly arrive there and access your:

- Blog?
- Twitter feed?
- Facebook identity?
- YouTube channel?

If not, you're making it harder—not easier—for them to discover you.

You also need to be aware of the keywords you're using. Are they driving people to your site because folks are looking for a particular topic, resource, product, or service? Getting creative with titles and topics is fine, but always keep in mind that you're creating content to drive traffic. Make sure that you carefully include your specialties—metal, plastics, refinery, oil, gas, machinery, hinges, widgets, whatever—in the way you title, position, title, and categorize your content.

The Second Stage of Awareness: Research

It's nice to think that all our customers are out there actively looking for us, but the fact remains that our customers are only looking out for themselves. Of course, that's as it should be. They have needs that we hope to satisfy.

As part of their needs, prospects will often research not companies, per se, but information (safety, protocol, options, materials, strengths, weaknesses, product grades, etc.).

Here is where your white papers, e-books, and articles come in handy. Creating a wide variety of content over a series of topics that we know, through research, our customers are looking for, are interested in, and can use helps us help them.

Get in databases. List your e-books where people can find them. Submit articles to the most popular, respected, and recognized trade journals, websites, and other publications. Offer your e-book on Amazon.com, Smashwords.com, iTunes, etc.

Don't just create content and let it gather dust. Get active about promoting your content as well.

The Third Stage of Awareness: Sourcing

As the stages of awareness trickle down to decision-making time, we reach our third stage, or sourcing. In the sourcing stage, customers know you. They are aware of you. The want to know you better and become more aware of you.

They know your name, have possibly bookmarked your website for future reference, and are familiar with the surface layers of your product offerings. Now it's time for them to dig deeper; make it easier for them.

This is where your CEO's blog will bring more of your company's personality to light. Your daily tweets or what you choose to share on Facebook will fine-tune what folks think about you. Your opinions matter; in this stage, they are both personal and professional.

The Fourth Stage of Awareness: Procurement

An often underappreciated aspect of content is how you choose to write up the mundane, the regular, and the everyday. Your product descriptions, catalog copy, and the captions you use to denote a certain item or item number can be considered content.

While your customers may not be in the mood for creatively "cutesy" product descriptions, there are still ways to make this content come alive in a way that is personal to your customers and makes their trip to your website simpler, faster, and more effective for their needs.

Pay attention to how products are categorized. Is it the easiest thing to follow? Do the links work? Where do they send people? Do they have to back up six clicks to get where they want—or can the page design quickly and easily point them more closely to where they need to go?

Creating quality content and pouring it into a shoddy or fractured web design process is one sure way to see that not only is it wasted, but this fourth and critical phase of awareness—procurement—is wasted as well.

Parting Words about Content Inventory

Remember that it's all about content. Every time you hear some expert or consultant or competitor talking about Facebook shares or tweets or website statistics or media impressions, think about content. All the technology in the world, all the gizmos and gadgets, the websites and the users, won't mean squat if they're not used as platforms to promote your content. So often in industrial manufacturing, marketing and promotion is the means *and* the end.

Now you have a clear goal in mind.

What are you marketing? Content.

What are you promoting? Content.

CHAPTER 6

Industrial Blogs—The Modern Trade Journal

Another shift from traditional media to web media has been the sudden and unprecedented rise of companies creating blogs for a variety of reasons, audiences, and messages. Regardless of the industry you serve or the companies/consumers you cater to, building a better blog is a necessity in today's demanding social media scene.

As an industrial marketing tool, blogs are a great symbol of the social, personal, unique, and interactive way that modern consumers demand the information they need. Thanks to their personal nature and immediacy, these blogs have risen to such status and usefulness that they have replaced and become the modern trade journal.

Unlike a traditional trade journal, however, or even a well-placed article and editorial, blogs give industrial marketers much more control of—and access to—their message, while providing a more interactive reading experience for the end user. Industrial marketers must understand how to utilize this outlet for a variety of purposes.

The More the Merrier

Blogging can build an online community of avid fans, followers, and subscribers—and it's a great way to bring the company together as a cohesive unit. Share the blogging duties. Many blogs regularly feature a revolving cast of bloggers. Susie every Monday, Ralph every Thursday, and Bill every second Wednesday.

Having other employees regularly blog can become a companywide activity, giving employees a voice to the community. Inviting employees to contribute empowers them and gives your blog a wider range of scope as well. You may even offer an individual blog to employees whose blogs are the most entertaining or are followed by the most people.

Blogging by the Keyword

According to Hubspot.com, "B2C companies that blog get 88 percent more leads/month than those who don't." B2B companies that blog get 67 percent more leads a month. These are only a few ways in which blogging has become the new trade journal and, by default, one of the more controllable aspects of industrial manufacturing marketing.

Unlike a single article that gets printed—often months after it was written—blogs allow you daily, hourly access to the most popular keywords that affect your business. Be it safety, market share, bandwidth, a new material, a new lubricant, a new trend, or a new focus, blogs offer new opportunities for keyword targeting. Every blog post is a new marketing opportunity to target new, non-branded keywords that can drive industrial traffic to your website. Your website will pull in branded keywords; your blog should focus on non-branded keywords.

Find out what's being talked about—and talk about it consistently, with authority, using compelling facts, anecdotes, language, and the keyword in question.

People talk about keywords a lot because they matter. They work. They drive traffic to your site; this traffic might not be there if not for searching for a particular keyword, finding your blog post about it, and clicking the link. Imagine more people clicking that link more often—and then imagine how to do it without a blog.

If you treat it seriously and serve up new, targeted content continuously, your company blog puts in you control of the content and your business growth.

Blogs Last a Lifetime

Another great thing about blogging is that they last. This is one of the biggest differences between traditional and new media. Traditionally, you put out an ad in a trade journal, and it was no longer valuable once the next issue came out. The chances of someone reaching for an old issue and seeing your ad once the new issue was in their hands was close to nil.

Today, it's the norm. Blog posts are continually repurposed, cross-linked, double-checked, and googled. Let's say you write a great blog post about the new material you're using to extend the lifespan of your company's brass door hinges, and let's say the name of this material is "xanthanite quadratus."

Every time someone searches for that keyword, "xanthanite quadratus," your blog has the potential to appear. The more people look at that post, read it, respond to it, comment on it, share it, link to it, tweet it, or repost it on Facebook, the higher its visibility. There is no telling how popular that post could get—and it lasts as long as the Internet does. One, two, three years later, it's still being linked to whenever anyone searches for "xanthanite quadratus."

As long as the article is well written, keyword rich, illustrative, entertaining, or educational, it has a good chance of being read years later. This isn't just a fantasy; it's a reality that happens for many companies who blog every day.

Ten Tips for Building a Better Blog

From expanding the size and content of your website (allowing for more opportunities to gain search engine rankings) to turning frequently asked questions into ongoing blog posts, blogs are here for the long haul and provide a variety of advantages to industrial companies.

Here are ten simple but effective tips for building a better blog without breaking the bank:

Post with purpose. No one has time for flabby, lethargic, uninteresting, and loosely targeted blogs—not you, the author, or your consumers, the readers. So post with purpose. Write with your target audience in mind; before you post anything, ask yourself six simple questions:

- Is this informative?
- Is it entertaining?
- Is it useful?
- Is it targeted?
- Does it align with our overall brand message?
- Will it motivate readers to comment on it?

If your post doesn't answer at least three of those items in the positive, go back to the drawing board and rewrite it until it does!

Integration is your motivation. The blog should not be the red-headed stepchild of your promotional strategy or the A-list star. It should be integrated, on point, and on message with all your marketing materials—from traditional to new media and from print to web and beyond.

As with each "arm" of your promotional efforts, the blog shouldn't be a random, entirely creative, or personal exercise. It should be purposeful and strategic.

Look at a calendar and figure out how often you're going to blog. If it's twice a week, great. What are you going to say each week? Have a list of topics to discuss, discuss them in order, and in a way that invites readers to come back each week.

Determine how—and where—the blog fits with your other marketing materials. Don't do double duty. If, for instance, you plan on writing an e-book on industrial safety or a white paper on current industry trends or some other topic of interest to your readers, post similar topics in the weeks leading up to, during, and beyond the e-book or white paper's release.

Of course, this is just one example of how to integrate the blog with your other promotional efforts. The goal is to have several "spokes" of marketing materials appearing regularly—from tweets to forums to Facebook updates to e-books and articles and beyond—with the blog as the hub that links them all together. When you think of integration that way, it's easy to see how vital a blog is to your organization's success.

Frequency matters. Research indicates that companies who blog over a dozen times per month get twice as much traffic as those companies who blog half as much. There is no secret formula for posting metrics, but clearly posting once or twice a month isn't going to produce the ROI you're looking for, given the amount of time it takes to post that often.

Here are some ways to increase the frequency of your posts without writing that much more additional content:

- Invite other employees to blog with you.
- Give one or two employees a regular column on your blog—or their own blog.
- Divide longer blogs into a series of shorter ones. So if you write eight hundred words on "The Four Ways to Increase Plant Safety," don't post all eight hundred on Monday. Post the first part on Monday, the second part on Wednesday, the third part on Friday, and so on.
- Serialize your posts. Go into a post knowing you're going to split it up. Purposefully try to find ways to string one post into two, three, five, or even six smaller posts.

Have a Dialogue—Not a Monologue

Blogging is an invitation for others to communicate with you. In an article or editorial, you post a statement and walk away. If it's printed, there never was any opportunity for readers to comment. Even if it appears on a professional journal's website, you have no control over how the comments or handled—or even if they're turned on or not.

A blog is your baby; you write it, you own it, you post it, and you're in a position to engage directly with your readers by writing informally, as a friendly and nurturing narrator who has all the answers and plenty of time to share them. Ask questions, discuss recent trends, invite participation, and spend as much time responding to questions, comments, queries, and complaints as you do blogging.

Many bloggers see blogging as a different mechanism for delivering speeches, editorials, or articles, but that's not what blogging is at all. Where traditional publishing was focused from the writer to the reader, social media publishing is directed from the writer to the reader and back again. This "back again" component is the most critical differential between blogging and writing articles.

Demonstrate Your Expertise

There is no sense in being a wishy-washy blogger! By all means, invite reader participation, welcome comments, and quote liberally from others. But make no mistake that the purpose of this blog is to communicate your—and your company's—expertise on all things industrial manufacturing.

Whatever topic you address—from safety to industry-specific material to future trends to the weather—do it with authority and absolute conviction. The way to make your blog rise above the rest is to have an opinion, to have convictions, and to have—and share your—expertise.

Don't see your blog as another chore or duty. It is a chance to build a resource library of timely, expert, and significant pieces that can be endlessly linked to. It will drive traffic to your company and close the sales loop for your loyal—or first-time—readers.

Make it Personal

Although I often call blogs the new trade journals, one of the many differences between those two forms of publication is that blogging is extremely personal. Think of the blogs you follow and how you develop a close relationship with the blogger. You look forward to his posts, love her sense of humor, and comment frequently—or would like to.

Assume that readers will bookmark you and visit regularly—and write accordingly. Have opinions, share anecdotes, and do all the things that your favorite bloggers do—only infuse it with your own style. This is not to say that you should copy or even emulate others to the point where you lose yourself. Maybe your favorite bloggers are fun, irreverent cheerleaders—even though that's the opposite of your style. Don't imitate. Being personal means being yourself.

Some of my favorite blogs are written by curmudgeons who have me rolling on the floor laughing with their get-off-my-lawn antics even as they use them to make salient, useful, and even strategic points about industrial manufacturing. The only way to share what you know to maximum effect is to share it while using your own personal style.

Comments Are Open

Ignore the interactive and ever-changing comments section of your blog at your own peril. These comments are unsolicited and can be invaluable nuggets of wisdom, frustration, insight, and urgency that no focus group could uncover.

To blog is to converse, not broadcast. The comments section is where your readers "talk back to you." Not every comment is productive, but all comments speak to you in some form or fashion. For instance, you know you're really hitting on a topic of interest when the amount of comments mushrooms. Maybe you're used to getting only a dozen or so on a typical blog post, but suddenly this week's post finds that number tripling, quadrupling, or more. Revisit what you talked about—and what the commenters had to say—and write more along those lines. I'm not saying to completely write what the comments dictate, but it's a wasted opportunity not to respond to them.

Speaking of responses, always respond to your blog comments—always. Some of the strongest business relationships I've ever formed started out as commenters on my blog—and they have become close allies and occasionally even friends.

Repurpose Content

It can be daunting to create new material every week, particularly since blogging is an integral part of your social media strategy, but that integration will also be your salvation. For instance, your blog posts can become the content for your e-books, white papers, etc.

If you've written a great white paper that contains a short section on an industry-specific topic, summarize it—or excerpt it—and post it as a blog. Likewise, if you've written a great blog post about a topic that ties in with your upcoming white paper or e-book, use it there as well. The beauty of blogging yourself is that you own all the content and can repurpose it in any way you see fit.

Rise above the Noise

It may seem daunting to even get into the social media scene at this point since so much of the field is already glutted with content, Facebook pages, and websites. When it gets noisier, it is an opportunity to rise above the clatter and make your voice heard.

Measurements Matter

Finally, use whichever blog format you utilize—Blogger.com, Wordpad, etc.—and mine their analytics to see now how each blog post performs. If possible, find out why. If there's a spike, go to the comments section and see what people are saying.

If you've written on a topic several times, but it just falls flat each time, cross that topic off your list and move on to something else. If you know that a certain topic or newsworthy event always doubles or triples your hits, return to that well to explore it deeper.

Blog measurements are like instant feedback on your performance. They help you avoid writing about content your audience isn't interested in—while writing more about the topics that do interest them.

Promoting Your Blog

We want results—not a library of random, mostly useless blog posts. Part of building a blog—to say nothing of stocking it with fresh, relevant content—is to promote it actively.

We could spend an entire book talking about promoting your blog. Many authors already have. But I would be remiss in writing a chapter on blogging without at least sharing a few simple tips about how to help promote your blog:

- **Make it easy to share:** Be sure to make it easy for others to promote your blog for you. Social media is such that if you offer relevant, timely, useful, and keyword-driven blog posts, others will want to share your expertise in lieu of, or to certify, their own. Make sure that each blog post has simple buttons where, with a mouse click, readers can like it on Facebook, share it on Facebook, tweet it, and use any other form of social media sharing they want to do.

- **Run a giveaway or contest:** Giveaways and contests are great calls to action—and great invitations to read, follow, join, and participate in your blog. Particularly when you create your own content, such as an e-book or white paper, you can give these away with little to no cost to yourself, but plenty of benefit to the reader. You can run a contest that offers the winner a thirty-minute call with your marketing department, VP, CEO, etc.

- **Mix it up:** Offer a variety of content on the blog—a video blog for one post, a podcast for the next, and a series of pictures in another blog, interspersed with your usual written posts. Different readers will respond better to videos, audio, or pictures. If you can provide variety for your readers, you can reach—and sell to—more customers.

- **Get noticed:** One of the best ways to promote your blog is to make it promotable. Have a clear, distinct, recognizable design. Have a logo, a familiar blog name, or a banner at the top that is easily reproduced and used and noticed when you—or others—share it. So much of success has to do with being prepared for success. Look at your favorite blogs; pay attention to what works for them. Try to remember how you ran across them, what worked, what didn't—and then replicate it.

- **Get creative with content:** Gimmicks may get you noticed, but quality keeps them coming back. If you run a giveaway and have mediocre content, folks may come once, but what's their incentive to return, other than another giveaway? Create quality content with a unique, creative flair that stands out among the daily alerts, subscriptions, e-mails, and notices your followers get. Use meaningful statistics, compelling titles, popular keywords no one else is writing about, and a style that is unequivocally yours. One of the most overlooked aspects of promoting a blog is also the simplest: *Don't just give them a reason to come—give them a reason to come back.*

- **Share and share alike:** The beauty of having a blog, a Twitter page, a Facebook page, and a LinkedIn account is that you already have three built-in vehicles for sharing when you publish a new blog post. When your new post goes up, tweet about it to your followers. Share it on Facebook with your hundreds—or thousands—of Facebook friends or fans. Share it with your LinkedIn community—and with every community you belong to. Set up your Twitter, Facebook, LinkedIn, and other social media platform settings so that the posts automatically hit all points at once.

Generating Leads from Your Blog

Blog with a purpose. Every blog should have dedicated calls to action to drive readers into the sales cycle. Get them to download your e-book, subscribe to your newsletter, contact a sales representative, sign up for a course, show up at an event, win a contest, or take a survey. As creative, consistent, and entertaining as your blog may be, never forget that it exists to engage people in the sales cycle.

Industrial blogging is not a company news page. It should focus on delivering valuable content to the audience. FAQs are a great place to start.

The industrial world isn't going to be engaging with other bloggers, guest bloggers, etc. That's the difference between industrial and consumer-based blogging. Industrial blogs are at a different stage of the sales cycle than consumer-based blogs used to generate new leads, etc.

Industrial blogs should be used in the discovery stage of the sales cycle, but they add the most value in the research phase because industrial buyers will typically know their requirements when searching for information on specific products.

Parting Words about Blogging

While more time and creativity intensive than the more traditional turnkey banner ads or direct mail campaigns of old, blogging is social media's answer to creating a personal, professional, expert brand on the Internet.

The strategies listed here are simple, if not exactly easy. Used as a basis for any blog launch, with growth, experience, and understanding, you will likely add to them, layer them, blend them, and utilize them in your own way.

And that's what blogging's all about.

CHAPTER 7

Searching for Industrial Products? Google It!

Traditional marketing media has changed—irrevocably and forever.

When folks were in the market for your industrial manufacturing product, they would usually be aware about it via some source of traditional industrial marketing media, such as branding in trade journals or print advertising, or they would look you up in that old standby, the Yellow Pages (or another industry-specific directory).

Print advertising is on the decline, and the Yellow Pages and other traditionally printed directories are barely breathing. According to Stateofthemedia.org, the "traditional [print newspaper] advertising pool declined for a sixth consecutive year." Meanwhile, the Publishers Information Bureau (PIB) stated that magazine rate card advertising suffered an "18.1 percent decline against the previous year."

And, speaking on behalf of search engine technology versus the Yellow Pages, Bill Gates said, "Yellow Page usage amongst people in their, say below 50, will drop to near zero over the next five years" (http://www.webtrafficpartners.com/yellow-pages-decline.html).

Thanks to the Internet, in general, and search engines like Yahoo, Bing, and Google in particular, companies no longer have to spend the lion's share of their advertising dollars being listed in expensive print catalogs, journals, and directories. They can maximize their industrial marketing dollars by being where it matters most—on the web, in real time, where current and future leads are already lurking.

Why SEO?

You hear so much about Search Engine Optimization (SEO) because it's effective. The average keyword search is going to return thousands, tens of thousands, even hundreds of thousands of hits during an average keyword search.

Depending on what site you're using—from Yahoo to Amazon to Bing to Goodreads to Google—you're only going to get about a dozen responses to any keyword on the vital first page, where the majority of business decisions are made.

If you're a commercial property manager in charge of overseeing hundreds of thousands of square feet and need a reliable, dependable air sanitation system for the thousands of restrooms in your domain, where are you going to start? If you're unhappy with your local supplier or the company you've been using hasn't been getting the job done, you're likely going to start from scratch and that means hitting up Google and keying in something like "industrial restroom supplies" or "aerosol restroom system" or "air freshener."

If you're busy, on a budget, and strapped for emotional and professional bandwidth, your search will likely be focused solely on those first ten or twelve results. Maybe you'll drift past the first page—but likely not much farther.

The "race for space" has become more competitive and challenging as more industrial manufacturing firms in your target area of business compete for those first ten, twelve, fifteen, eighteen, or twenty slots.

How do you get noticed? Google, Yahoo, Bing, and AOL use a series of metrics (which I won't go into here) to move various keyword results up or down. Basically, those metrics rely on a series of variables like *linkability* (how many other sites is your blog, website, web page, article, or e-book linked to), *relevance* (how relevant are the keywords on your blog, website, or product listing compared to the actual search term used), *popularity* (back to linkability and who is talking about you in forums, blogs, etc.) and *availability* (obviously a dead page or bad link drops you back down) to arrive at those top results.

Choose Your Keywords Well

We've talked about your website, revamping your website or website copy, and even starting your own or a company blog, but we need to talk about the importance of the keywords you use in those structures.

Our main concern when starting an industrial manufacturing website should be capturing and closing leads—period. That's what all of this is about. Part of that process is understanding how prospects come across you. Since so much has changed in the last ten years, it's imperative to keep the end user in mind as much as possible while presenting the information they need to make informed purchasing decisions.

On any given web page, you have four critical opportunities to make it what industry experts call "keyword rich."

- **The web page's URL:** The link that will appear in the user's browser.
- **The text title of the web page:** The title of the web page as it appears in the top of the user's web browser.
- **The description in the meta tag:** How you describe what's on the page where readers can't see it (for web programmers only).
- **Throughout the content on the page itself:** This could include what you say in your blog post, the letter from your CEO, the product description of a brass fitting, valve, pipe, gasket or gear, quotes from satisfied customers, etc.

Since I don't expect you to be a computer programmer, webmaster, or actually sit at your desk and think of every keyword for every page yourself, I'll focus on what I think is most critical for the average industrial manufacturing CEO, VP, or marketer: turning your content into keyword-rich wordsmithing that sells.

Now and Then: The Concept of Short- and Long Tail Keywords

You've probably heard the terms "short tail" and "long tail" thrown out around the web. They are extremely important to understand when it comes to keywords.

As you might imagine, there are all kinds of different keywords out there. Some are simple, like "toilet" or "gear shaft," while others are more complicated and distinct, like "low-flow toilet with prestandard fittings" or "metal alloy gear shaft for large machinery."

Depending on what type of search a person is engaging in, be it starting from scratch or narrowing down his choices, he is more likely to respond to a short- or long-tail keyword. So, for instance, if I'm a general contractor just starting my search, I'm going to start with a simple, short-tail keyword like "toilet" or "plumbing." If I'm farther along in my search, I may know that I need a more specific keyword to narrow the choices of companies I'll be ordering from, such as "low-flow toilet with prestandard fittings."

Here is how we might apply the concept of short- and long-tail to writing keywords for your web copy:

- **Short-tail** keywords are general, direct, obvious, and practical for early searchers who may want to sample a wide variety of vendors. Early in the search, short-tail keywords are practical because they can give a broad scope, or picture, of what's out there.
- **Long-tail** keywords will help establish your industrial manufacturing firm as the "go-to" source for whatever folks come to you for. Generally, the more keywords that are specific to your product, such as "low-flow toilet with

prestandard fittings" is going to translate into long-tail keywords. They're called long-tail because while first-time users may not find you this way, those that are farther along in their search and closer to making a purchasing decision will use them to narrow their choices to one or two vendors.

Let's revisit our earlier example of a busy, urban property manager looking to score a safe, practical, quick, simple, and affordable solution to keeping his 2,689 restrooms fresh and pleasant for his commercial property clients.

A short-tail list of keywords you can use to capture this prospect's attention during his or her initial search might include things like these keywords:

- air fresheners
- bathroom cleaners
- deodorizers
- restroom smells

These are examples of short-tail keywords. They will product high traffic (hence the term, short-tail), but they may not result in immediate sales or even click-throughs because these obvious, logical, almost blunt keyword opportunities tend to attract first-time searchers—not ready-to-be-buyers.

These keywords would become difficult to optimize for the search engines, requiring much more effort, traffic, and competition to profit from them.

You want to establish your expertise across the industry. You want to attract brand-loyal consumers with your white papers, e-books, blog posts, and additional content. You want to become a thought leader in your industry, the go-to website, blog, or resource when folks are looking for whatever you offer.

Certain long-tail keywords are going to be easier to rank on search engines because of the specificity of the search and lack of competition. These long-tail keyword opportunities allow quick search engine results. Although they will return less traffic than short-tail keywords, they will produce much more targeted and industry-specific traffic because those who find your site by using them are searching exactly for what you're optimizing for. Short-tail keywords will return higher traffic—and sometimes much broader audiences that may not always be targeted to the search.

- experts in fresh restroom aromas
- neutralizing scents
- air-freshening solutions for property managers

You can see how these keywords might appeal to a more discriminating, more thoughtful, more serious end user, which can help secure serious consumer leads and attract attention from national and local media, other thought leaders, business partners, and additional industry-specific opportunities.

The Blend: Your Secret to Keyword Rich Copy That Sells!

One of the first temptations of learning, and adopting, SEO as a marketing strategy is to pick a few industry keywords—*gasket, seal, bearing,* or *air freshener*—and use it to death. Use it in the URL: www.manufacturingsolutions.com/gaskets. Use it in the page title "Gaskets and More Gaskets." Use it in the meta tags the consumer can't see: "a web page about gaskets, precision gaskets, heat sensitive gaskets, etc." And, worst of all, using it in the text ad nauseum until it's barely readable:

> Our gaskets are indomitable. No other gaskets perform like these gaskets in the history of gaskets. When you use one of our gaskets, all your gasket problems will be solved.

But search engine metrics are becoming increasingly sensitive to such "SEO overload," and keywords are not the only considerations that push your page higher in the search site rankings.

You want your copy be keyword rich and link friendly, so that other sites, databases, users, bloggers, reviewers, and industry journalists will link to it heavily—and no one will link to an SEO-generated page that reads like an industrial manufacturing Mad Lib!

Instead of focusing on an avalanche of keywords, blend them in naturally—in ways that are germane to what you're talking about and helpful to the reader as "road signs" for why they're looking at your website, blog, e-book, or white paper in the first place.

Let's take a page from some actual copy that might appear on a random web page from an average industrial cleanser company about its restroom freshening products:

> The air freshening properties of Insurgent Corp's "Restroom Relief" line of bathroom cleansing solutions offers trusted relief from the most persistent restroom odors with patented protection you can trust. A variety of pleasant scents, such as winter lilac and summer strawberry, are periodically released every six minutes to statistically reduce the amount of odors experienced by your restroom users.

See how the keywords are still there, but pop more because they make sense, fit logically, and actually work toward a logical conclusion? In all things SEO, focus on the keywords—but also focus on the blend that makes them stand out all the more for their usefulness and appropriateness.

Catch and Capture: Making Your Website More Effective

SEO isn't—and shouldn't be—an isolated, creative effort *unto itself.* What you're doing with SEO is attracting first-time, second-time, and long-time users to your website through a variety of carefully brainstormed, carefully captured keywords. But what will they do when they get there?

We said one major boost to your website's search engine rankings remains its linkability, the invisible ranking boost that comes from other websites linking to yours via your website, articles, white papers, e-books, blog, etc.

There are three main types of links:

1.) **Authoritative:** These links are the best type in terms of search engine rankings because they come from authority sites such as .gov or .edu sites. The more respectable the site the link comes from, the more value the search engines give it.

2.) **Topical:** These are good/okay links because they come from relevant sources that are related to the same topic as yours.

3.) **Reciprocal:** These are the "you link to me, I like to you" links. They are the least effective in terms of search engine rankings—and in terms of a linking strategy. Google's evolution has made this type of linking irrelevant.

One way to make your website not only keyword rich but ultimately linkable is to practice what I call the "catch-and-capture" message. Here are some simple tips to do just that:

- **Create captivating titles:** Titles are a golden, and often overlooked, opportunity to take SEO to the next level. Every piece of copy on your website should have a title. A blog post? Title. Catalog description of twelve different types of rubber seals? A title for each one. Even subtitles can be helpful to focus readers and make a page more keyword rich. For instance, let's say your "About Us" page is six paragraphs long. If you break it up into three sections with two paragraphs each, and have a subtitle for each two-paragraph section, you can find additional ways to appropriately enrich that page with additional targeted keywords.

- **Write backward:** The key to linkability is keeping things short, sweet, and to the point. Everyone is hip to SEO now, and that makes it harder than ever to be linkable if you're writing for SEO's sake. So don't. Look at your creative marketing as the cake and the SEO as the icing—not the other way around. If you find it a challenge to write—or have your team write—new creative material without being too SEO, write the piece first without worrying about any keywords and then go back through it with a specific eye for SEO. Sometimes "writing backward" like this can help you put the writing first and the keywords second.

- **Make it likeable to make it linkable:** Sometimes you have to ignore the tips, strategies, and tactics and just strip linkability down to its most basic core. For instance, why do you link to something? Typically, it's because the content is such that you know your readers would find it as useful, valuable, and linkable as you do. Start backward and work to that. Write unique, creative, knowledgeable, expert, useable content that people will want to link to because they know it's authoritative, valuable, and useful for their readers.

- **Have a site map:** Site maps allow end users to find information on your site more easily, and they increase the chances of various keyword-rich categories being linked to quickly and often. They increase the amount of keywords per page when based at the bottom of the page and are stationary/static whenever the page changes.

- **Focus on quality:** Above all, keywords are accessories—not content. Many companies make the mistake of flipping that order and writing content around the keywords. Don't fall into that trap. Always produce great, quality content that is accentuated with keywords—not the other way around!

Avoiding Black Hat Tactics: A Word to the Wise

You'll notice in this chapter that the types of SEO and link-encouragement I recommend are all straight-up, above-the-board practices. While these may mean more work for you and your staff, the payoff is in knowing that the keyword terms you're using are sound—and the links you get as a result are bona fide.

Of course, there will always be companies looking for shortcuts to success; several big-name companies have done so at the cost of bad publicity. In several cases, they have been banned from the mother of all search engines—Google.

JC Penney and Overstock.com, among other companies, have been busted by Google for buying links, a little known but common practice in the world of SEO tactics and strategies. Before you start scratching your heads and wondering what's so wrong with that, know that buying links is not the same as buying (paid) advertising.

Instead, buying links is done to specifically elevate a company's search engine rankings in a false and misleading manner. Many of the bought links appear on pages with nothing but other links; they have clearly been designed to manipulate the search engines into seeing tons of links for a certain topic, company, brand, etc. When Google found out that JC Penney—or the SEO company they had hired to help them attain high search engine rankings—was paying for links and manipulating the system, they were promptly banned from Google.

As you might imagine, if Google was important enough to try to manipulate in the first place, being kicked off the world's most popular search engine is a costly, embarrassing, reputation-stinging, and bottom-line-busting business blunder.

If you don't want to make it yourself, don't fall victim to so-called black hat tactics as buying links or other unscrupulous SEO behavior. Do it the old-fashioned way: work hard, get creative, and be better at SEO than the other guy—not just sneakier.

SEO Is Constantly Evolving. Are You?

I hesitate to close the door on this chapter because I know, by the time I do, some new brilliant SEO twist will pop up on my radar. SEO is constantly evolving—and so must you.

As you begin to see results with your SEO marketing, learn the best way to measure results so you can fine-tune your process to focus on what works. Become an SEO student by subscribing to top writers on the subject, following their blogs, and frequently being alerted via Google Alerts to new writings on the topic.

Groom your marketing staff in the benefits of SEO to ensure that they—and your marketing efforts—constantly evolve as well. Learning the benefits of SEO early—and using them often—is a great way to improve your web content and begin reaping its benefits ASAP.

Parting Words: Adapting SEO for Industrial Marketing

The beauty, and danger, of industrial marketing is that it's so targeted and specific. This makes SEO a valuable marketing tool; however, unlike other industries that exist purely online, you can't make it your only marketing tool.

SEO is just one aspect of how you should market your industrial manufacturing business. Indeed, without many of the other tools we've already mentioned—your website, your blog, etc.—SEO drives new visitors to old messages.

CHAPTER 8

Managing Your Online Reputation

One of the biggest struggles in dealing with the burgeoning world of online marketing is the anonymous, occasionally angry world of Internet commenters. Obviously, there have always been dissatisfied customers throughout the history of industrial marketing, but in the golden age of traditional advertising, it took a lot more work for customers to complain to you—let alone *about* you.

Back then, most disgruntled customers had to actually pick up the phone and dial a customer service representative at your toll-free number or write you a letter. If they were a big enough client, they could schedule a meeting.

Today, in two clicks or less, anyone—consumer or not, satisfied or not, random stranger or longtime customer—can write pretty much anything they want to say about you in an increasing variety of places—in ways that could potentially damage your business, brand, or reputation.

From Yelp! to Amazon, from your own blog to your website, even on their own blogs or websites, consumers are increasingly venting their frustrations about companies by blasting them online. What's more, companies are finding it increasingly challenging to undo the damage even one disgruntled consumer can do online.

Even gigantic companies like Bic are seemingly powerless against the whims of the online mob. They probably spent years and countless millions designing a line of pens specifically for women. Shortly after their "For Her" line of Bic Cristal pens became available online, they experienced an immediate, unprecedented, and ugly tidal wave of consumer contents, particularly on the massive e-tail website Amazon, where customer comments ranged from irate to ironic.

Even months after the kerfuffle occurred, those comments—1,621 and counting, for an average of three stars—are still on Amazon. While the minor Internet meme certainly won't do permanent damage, the launch of what was clearly designed to be a major line for Bic can clearly be seen as a disappointment.

For smaller companies—and even midsize to large companies—it can be a nightmare scenario to find an unflattering or negative portrayal of your company online. Imagine hearing from a customer or a prospect that upon looking at one of the search engines for information about your company, they saw extremely negative blog posts or forum entries.

And that's just from people kind enough to say something to you. One can only imagine the countless potential customers who were turned off and went elsewhere after seeing one too many—or even one—unflattering messages about you, your company, your brand, or a particular product or service.

Naturally, being alerted to negative online messages becomes instantly problematic as you immediately start to wonder:

- How long has the negative information been there?
- How damaging is what it says?
- What does it say?
- Where does it say it?
- Have others linked to it?
- How much traffic is in the site(s)?
- How many prospects (potentially) saw the information?

What Can You Do about It?

Amazingly, with the vastness of the Internet and the technology that currently exists, we are mostly powerless to prevent the critical opinions of others online. The worst part about seeing a substantially negative report is that there is little you will be able to do immediately to change it.

However, your industrial marketing plan must still account for this activity. And, since you really have no defense against customers complaining about bad products or services, your only real defense is a good offense—doing a better job of building an online reputation, plus stellar products and services, that folks won't want to complain about.

How People Think: The Ugly Edition

The anonymous nature of the Internet, including commenters using phony names or not having to leave a name, has given rise to a decidedly ugly trend in the evolution of consumer-commenting options. What started as a great way for consumers to share reviews and comments about everything from books (Amazon.com) and movies (RottenTomatoes.com) to technology (BestBuy.com) to restaurants (Yelp.com) to even the news (HuffingtonPost.com) has become, for many, a free-for-all where they can anonymously rant and rave to their heart's content.

These days, nearly every business has experiences with customers that end with a less than positive outcome. However, in the era of the Internet searching for information, some of those experiences don't necessarily end there. Instead, they sometimes—and quite often—end with

- a negative comment made about your company on a high authority blog,
- a negative rating on review sites such as Google Places, Amazon, etc., or

- a negative thread in a forum created for the purpose of discussing your company.

Above all, the Internet is a sticky place. Things have a way of sticking around forever—unflattering pictures, portraits, comments, or reviews of your company or brand. The problem with each of the above scenarios is that they are found in search results as relevant web pages describing your company. Anyone searching for background information on your business will see the negative report—often prominently and seemingly without any noticeable challenge to it. Of course, this type of negative commenting could put doubt, even serious doubt, in a potential client's mind before they consider working with you or your company.

Prevention is critical in this arena; any solid marketing for a manufacturing plan should take this into consideration and make plans to deal with it ahead of time.

What can a company do proactively to avoid this nightmare scenario? How can a company work with an industrial marketing consultant to make sure this does not damage potential goodwill with prospective customers?

Whether a company manager discovers the negativity online and needs to combat it—or understands its potential impact and wants to take steps to avoid it—the action taken will be the same. Unfortunately, there is not much that can be done quickly to change information (even if it is false) on someone's website.

The best course of action is to apply a forceful campaign of proactive and positive search engine optimization. The plan of attack can be described as the best defense is a good offense. Your company will displace or mitigate the effect of negative visible information with massive amounts of positive information.

Of course, steps should be taken to isolate and rectify particular incidents as they arise. Just as critically, steps should be taken daily, even habitually, to prevent incidents from arising in the first place.

Reputation Management in Five Easy Steps

The phenomenon of finding negative information about a company online certainly isn't new. In fact, the issue is so prevalent that there is an entire business model built around combating it called the "reputation management" industry. But apart from a few steps, reputation management is making sure that when it comes to your company's name, the information visible online speaks to things that enhance the image of your company.

Before you choose to hire someone to manage your reputation online, there are steps that you can and should take on behalf of your own company. Starting with making sure that your company's name online is safeguarded, here are five simple, active, and concrete steps to be taken to manage your company's reputation:

The First Step: Be Proactive about Social Media

Make sure that your company is using, in its own name, all of the available social media properties that can be found online. The major properties to start with are Facebook, LinkedIn, Twitter, Pinterest, Foursquare, YouTube, and Google Plus. Companies should make sure that any available business profiles are used. All of these platforms should have content populating the biographical area as completely as possible. Upload photos, leave no blanks unfilled, and fill them accurately, and thoroughly, with the positive history, impact, and aspects of your company.

Wherever there is information required regarding the company within these platforms, it should be completely filled in. Once this task has been completed for the major social networking platforms, most of these sites will begin to show as being "relevant" to your company's name during an Internet search.

Being proactive about the social media outlets available to you is helpful because it begins to populate the search engine results with outcomes you can predict and control—instead of leaving these sites dormant so that uglier, uncontrollable messages rise above them when prospects begin googling you.

The Second Step: Purposeful PR

Be purposeful, and predictable, with your PR. Public relations, now more than ever, is a critical factor in managing your online reputation, but many companies have turned from it because it is "too traditional." Instead, make sure that your company is submitting its news on a regular basis through news releases and press releases. Although the purpose of these releases is typically to get them noticed by the press, a number of them will remain online in the form of "news" when your company's name is searched.

Having news organizations and industry professionals link to your release will give it the kind of natural authority it needs to remain visible in search engines. The more often a company undertakes this strategy, the more opportunities it will have to occupy a visible position in search engine results.

The Third Step: Monitoring—and Responding to—Content

For companies that do business locally, it will be necessary to monitor review websites—as well as the Google business directory, called Google Places—for negative commentary from former customers. There is very little that you will be able to do to remove negative information. However, you *will* want to publicly respond to complaints.

Many companies feel they shouldn't "stoop" to responding to online consumer complaints—or that responding will only "validate" what the consumer has said—but saying nothing has been proven to be as counterproductive as responding with the wrong message. Instead, respond promptly, personally, and as positively as possible.

Being proactive about responding to online consumer complaints, no matter how valid or invalid, will demonstrate to future clients that you are conscientious and that you care about your business's reputation. Google actually provides guidelines for how a company should respond, which serves as excellent advice for responding to negative feedback on any review site.

The Fourth Step: Natural Link Building

Work with your industrial marketing consultant on what is known as a "natural" link-building campaign. You want search engines to view the links to your website as natural, content-based links. Never pay or exchange links with your link targets. When working with an agency, you will need to make sure that the contractor understands that the objective is not to have all sites rank at all costs. An overly aggressive campaign can lead to more penalties than benefits.

This content marketing campaign should not be viewed as a short-term process. The process should be a long-term project that will promote an accurate picture of the company's online reputation.

The Fifth Step: Rinse, Lather, and Repeat!

As you move forward in your industrial marketing efforts proactively and defensively, make it a habit to repeat these first four steps for all key executives and signature products of the company.

Creativity Is Key to Content Marketing

Making sure there is content in the locations where Internet users are likely to look for information about the company is paramount to managing its reputation proactively. Typically these five steps, if treated habitually and practiced regularly, will be sufficient for most companies—without having to hire a reputation management consultant. Every company, regardless of size, needs to have content strategies that require consistent additions to its online profile.

Content marketing and reputation management are closely related—and both are necessary for any company with a web presence. Does your company have a plan in place to deal with negative listings? Is your business acting proactively to create content to supplant potentially damaging information? If not, you may be leaving yourself open to letting the consumers manage your reputation rather than doing it yourself.

PART
3

Engaging Your Industrial Audience

CHAPTER 9

Content and Interaction Marketing

Sell. Sell. Sell. That was the fundamental marketing principle for most companies at one time. Basically, in the heydays and prime time of traditional, one-way marketing, what companies said went, and buyers were left to believe them until they found a reason not to.

We believed it if a laundry detergent said it was "new and improved," whether or not we saw any noticeable improvement ourselves. We believed it if companies made it seem like smoking was glamorous and drinking was elegant.

Today? Not so much. Rather than trusting some high-priced Madison Avenue advertising agency, or even the company they're working for when it comes to products and services, we're far more likely to trust the recommendations of our friends, families, neighbors, coworkers, and our online network of followers, friends, subscribers, and fans. It's telling over selling in a new wave of word-of-mouth advertising:

Fast-Forward Nation: Getting to the Good Stuff Has Never Been So Easy

There was a time when commercials were unavoidable in our lives. For many, they were a chance to get up from the couch and go get a snack, use the restroom, answer the phone, or stretch their legs. Others endured them, and the commercial messages seeped into popular consumer culture.

But look around today, and it will be quickly apparent that now living in "Fast-Forward Nation." Our culture no longer has the patience for commercials. Mentally, we fast-forward through them and do anything we can to avoid them. We endure them only when we have to—when we can't fast-forward them fast enough. That same mental calculus is taking place whenever a sales message is presented; they're all seen as commercials. And, just like televised commercials, the same mentality of mistrust is present when we hear preformed, calculated, creative sales messages.

Now more than ever, we are slightly distrustful of what a company has to say about itself, whether or not the message reaches us through a traditional salesperson, the traditional media, or the Internet.

People tend to be able to spot a viral video that's just a "fake" moment put on by a company that is trying to seem cool. We can spot ad copy a mile away, even if it sounds like everyday conversation, and we've been burned so many times by traditional marketing that our instant reaction is distrust and disbelief. We want to touch and experience the product or service and see it for ourselves; then we might believe what the company says.

"Prove It" Nation

The web, in general, and the user-generated content it has spawned, in particular, has created an expectation to be able to evaluate a sales message on our own, under our own steam, following our own instincts.

If somebody says, "Hey, look, we have great stuff," you say nothing in return. You might make a mental note or say, "We'll see." Or you'll race out of the store, storm the search engines, and make an objective decision on our own.

While this may not be the process by which someone comes to understand your brand, the effect is there when you are pouring your heart into how much your product will do for your clients. You're subtly saying, "Our stuff is cool." The prospects are subtly saying, "I don't trust you . . . yet."

This disconnect, this divide, is yours to cross. It's a bridge to getting the customer on your side by guiding them to that understanding in a unique, authentic, and user-controlled way.

Count Your Blessings . . . and Your Curses!

Marketing on the Internet is equal parts blessing *and* curse. It is a blessing because of the tremendous reach we have in communicating our message; it is a curse in that the modern mentality of a prospect is to hold up the buying process until they have had time to review your claims. If there was ever any emotive function in the buying process, it is dissipating as the Internet evolves. Prospects and clients want the entire truth—and they want it to be verified. They don't need or want the hype that companies have valued for so long.

The goal in moving forward with content-focused marketing is to embrace the blessing and turn away from the curse. Quit relying on the old-fashioned, traditional, one-way ad copy, which consumers are so openly distrustful of anyway, and focus on user-generated content: customer testimonials, interactive content like blog posts and comment sections, articles and posts and white papers and even books about the topics and materials you handle and how they're useful and where folks can find them.

Establish channels for distributing content and funneling feedback. Let consumers make their own decisions while gently guiding them via content *you* create—and *they* discover.

Content Marketing: It's All in How You Look at It

It doesn't have to be either/or. Marketing is still marketing, and it's not time to ditch your PR firm yet. You must take into account the new way consumers come to products; recognize it and innovate the way you market to be more telling than selling.

Savvy companies and marketers can use the web and the desire of customers to have facts verified to their advantage, by engaging in *content marketing*.

Content marketing can be a subjective term, but in its simplest sense, it is making facts about your products available and discoverable to lead prospects into your marketing funnel. It takes advantage of an aspect of human nature that makes us more trusting to solutions that we *discover ourselves* over those that are *presented to us*.

The Effectiveness of Content Marketing

Content marketing is effective because it resides where modern folks spend more of their time. Rather than dwelling in luxury sites like magazines and cable TV and billboards, it uses Internet channels, such as search engines, video marketing, and social media, to provide solutions to problems that exist in the everyday lives of prospects.

Content marketers make solutions available for clients and prospects to find in their organic search for solutions. Of course, that doesn't mean this is a hit-or-miss process. Content marketing doesn't mean you leave it all to chance, relying on customers to run across your information willy-nilly. In fact, marketers who do it well conduct research on where these problems are being discussed and pondered.

Are these problems being discussed in an industry-related forum? Are they being discussed in a social media group on Facebook or LinkedIn? Are they being queried on search engines (such as Google and Bing) or video sharing sites like YouTube?

A majority of the skill involved in successful, quality content marketing is finding out what the key questions are—and where they are being asked—and finding ways to provide answers at the source.

The Home Improvement Companies Get It

Home improvement companies, such as Lowe's and Home Depot, are light years ahead of other industries in performing content marketing that works consistently, reliably, and well. A simple Internet search for problems such as "how to fix a leaky faucet" will present a number of instructional videos of how a customer can undertake this venture.

A careful screening of the videos provides a couple of clues on the nature of content marketing and how it can be used successfully to help consumers solve problems—and be the ones to solve them:

- **The basis for the video is solving a problem, not to sell.** The "tell" comes before the "sell."
- **The companies in question (Lowe's and Home Depot) are transparent in their presentation.** They are not holding themselves out as the only place to solve the problem; they are offering a solution to the problem in a way that is simple and accessible to the consumer.

By providing content rather than advertising (even though, at heart, that's what it really is), the home improvement companies have successfully mapped the pain points of their target customers. They have provided quality, useful, standalone information—no "teaser" or "come visit us to find out the rest" endings here—to help them solve perplexing issues instead of selling them on how wonderful their store is.

This information is carefully targeted and strategically placed so it can be found by those who have the problem. Equally importantly, the information is formatted so it can be quickly and easily shared on the Internet with others who might have a similar problem.

Many marketers who go through the trouble of content marketing ignore the basic intent of this vehicle: quality information that is designed to be shared, disseminated, and spread across the web's new and emerging social features.

Lessons Learned

It all comes down to telling versus selling. Is there a better way to build a brand than to help a prospect—telling them how to do something, solve a problem, or find a solution—instead of selling them on how helpful you are? Can you associate your brand or your company as a solution-oriented partner when a prospect's problems are most mystifying to them?

Can you use the power of the Internet to be present when common problems are being discussed? If you can, you can overcome the human element of a prospect to distrust you when you need to state your call to action for them to buy. You can also build stronger relationships for the longer term.

You need to know the difference between telling and selling—and you must act on that difference. It's easier than ever to look like you're telling when, in actuality, you're really selling. Companies can focus on marketing buzzwords; SEO, social media, and inbound marketing are necessary. It is pretty easy to get a YouTube channel, a Facebook Fan page, or to pay someone to make you visible in search engines. Are you willing to use these channels in the way they were intended—in customer-oriented ways—before a sale is made? Are you willing to use them to position yourself as a problem solver without giving in to the temptation to "sell, sell, sell" while you're there? Are you willing to give your expertise, advice, and knowledge away for free—as Home Depot and Lowe's do with their videos—without expecting an immediate return on your investment?

If you are, if you can commit to the mentality that advertising is not a turnkey operation where you put in so many ad spend dollars in April and get them back in May, you will successfully embrace all the power the Internet has to help you to market your business.

Listen Closely: Clients Are Telling You How to Market to Them

With social media marketing becoming more rampant in today's society, companies are learning new ways to market to their clients. In fact, by using social media, clients are able to tell companies exactly how to market to them.

First, let's discuss a few ways that companies are using interaction marketing—and then we will discuss how they are using it to get clients to tell them exactly how to market to them.

Interaction Marketing: A Case Study in Content

In 2011, Jell-O created a campaign that marketed itself directly to Twitter users. It was called Jell-O Pudding Face. The company launched a website with a man's face on it. Through the website, they were able to track the "mood" of Twitter by tracking happy faces and sad faces contained in tweets. The more happy faces were posted, the happier the Jell-O face would become and the more sad faces that were posted on Twitter, the sadder the face.

When the face became very sad, Jell-O would give away free pudding to one of the sad tweeters. It was Jell-O's way of making the world a happier place. Plus, it was a great way to market and get its product out to customers and noncustomers alike.

This consumer-driven campaign was so special because it was thoroughly modern. The company didn't sell; it allowed users to "tell" it how they were feeling. On paper, this was little more than a giveaway promotion with free Jell-O being the "loss leader," but in reality it was a feel-good event that tapped into the interactivity and integrated marketing that is so popular with consumers today.

It touched them where they lived, online, and with what they were doing already anyway: tweeting and using emoticons. It was as random as it was thoroughly well planned, and it was executed beautifully. It was also simple and easily repeatable.

Now, let's look at Duck Tape Brand. For as long as duct tape has been around, it has been known as a fix-all. If you need something fixed, put duct tape on it. In recent years, some people have started to get crafty with duct tape. They started out making wallets and purses and such.

Duck Tape was paying attention. By seeing all of the crafty ideas suddenly appearing online, they began to ask consumers what they would like to see from the company. They had a huge response and started creating different colors of duct tape. The brand started holding contests to see how crafty people could get with their brand of tape. When prom dresses started showing up that were made completely with Duck Tape, the company started launching even more styles.

Now Duck Tape holds a yearly prom contest as well as contests to get ideas directly from consumers. That has helped them launch the Duck Tape club, a how-to site, and even Duck Tape with college logos. The company is continually interacting with its customers, plainly asking them what they want, and giving it to them. That's about as interactive as it gets!

How Clients Tell Companies What *Not* to Market to Them

Let's peek into our how-not-to-do-it files to see how interactivity looks when consumers see something marketed in the wrong way. In 2008, Motrin launched a large marketing campaign targeted to moms who carry babies in baby carriers. To paraphrase, it discussed how moms did it for fashion and to be considered a "good mom," and "oh by the way, it may help the baby to not cry as much. However, carrying the baby is very painful on your neck, back, and shoulders, so if you are a mom who uses a baby carrier, you should take Motrin."

This ad caused an uproar in the extremely volatile, extremely prolific "mommy blogging" arena. Many of the mom bloggers were tweeting criticism and causing a big stir online. Moms were not happy to be told that they were carrying their babies merely to benefit their reputations, and many voiced their disgust that Motrin would be so judgmental in something as silly as an aspirin ad.

Many also mentioned that if they were carrying or nursing their babies, Motrin was not something that they would be putting in their bodies to be transferred to their children in the first place. The mommy audience that Motrin was ultimately targeting felt that the company lacked the market research that they needed to campaign to the "mom" market in the first place—let alone the tact to market to it appropriately.

How did Motrin respond? At first, the company ignored all the criticism. But when it got to the point where it was undeniable, the company shut down its website and started sending out apologies to those who had e-mailed complaints. Motrin eventually relaunched its website, retracted the ad, and posted a formal apology on the website.

Had Motrin more closely monitored its reputation online, which is a lot simpler than it sounds, it would have been able to foresee the negative reaction—and would been able to take action *before it got out of control* and became a PR nightmare. The company could have individually responded to the few mom bloggers who initially noticed the ad and asked how they could improve.

Most consumers, given the chance, would be more than happy to let companies know what they want to see and what they expect from a company's marketing campaigns. It doesn't take much to invite consumer feedback, and your responses go a long way in undoing online damage—and preventing it in the future.

By tracking its reputation—and even the reputation of its competitors—a company can learn directly from its clients or prospective clients what they do not like and what problems need to be fixed in current marketing campaigns. I can't overstate the importance of such valuable information in this interactive, skeptical, and content-driven marketing environment.

Using this method—and bringing clients into the marketing campaigns with contests, giveaways, and polls—allows companies to have their clients tell them exactly how to market to them.

Or, in Motrin's case, how *not* to market to them. Knowing this information before committing to an online campaign—and the Internet can be very unforgiving—is priceless.

Parting Words about Content and Interaction Marketing

When your company knows exactly what your target market wants to see and what they don't want to see, it makes creating a campaign virtually foolproof.

And becoming a trusted source for content-driven marketing that is open and solicitous of consumer feedback makes it a brand they can trust not just for this purchase, but enough to make a second purchase and recommend that others do the same.

CHAPTER 10

Social Media Matters

Are you on social media? Are you convinced that if you're not toggling between Facebook and Twitter and 4Chan and Klout and Pinterest all day long, you're somehow missing the boat? Are you watching opportunities slip through your fingers? Is the world passing you by?

Well, the bad news is that you're partly right. The better news is that you're partly wrong! I don't recommend being on social media *unless you're going to use it!* Everyone and their mother, apparently, is suddenly an expert on social media—and they all claim that you absolutely *have* to be on social media 24/7 to survive, let alone succeed.

I disagree. I think having inactive social media accounts, such as where you have a Facebook fan page with only thirty-two likes or a Twitter account with only twenty-four followers hurts you worse than not being there at all because social media is all about the social. Think of it like a virtual conversation. When you're tweeting, throwing up a Facebook page, or posting pictures, you're basically talking to anyone who friends, follows, or subscribes to you.

Few things are worse, from a marketing perspective, than having someone reach out to you on a social media network—and to get nothing back.

It's the virtual version of someone calling you five times a day and you never picking up the phone, or snapping their fingers in your face to get your attention, only to receive a dazed look and the silent treatment in return. So, if you're not going to be fully dedicated to social media, either with manpower, attention, creativity, or concern, stay away from it altogether.

Unlike paying for ad space in an industrial catalog or trade periodical, social media is a giant, moving, hairy beast of an animal with a ton of working parts that, while not necessarily complicated, all require constant attention. It would be challenging for any book to cover everything you need to know to master social media, let alone one chapter. Clearly, this book is not designed to teach you everything there is to know about social media, but it introduces the B2B marketer to the many advantages of utilizing social media in the B2B space.

Many social media consultants focus their energy on helping companies engage with customers. In a business-to-consumer model, engagement often means conversations are designed to resolve problems or answer basic questions. However, in the business-to-business marketplace, social media success means much more than making small talk. The most successful B2B marketers focus on growing leads instead of counting likes.

Lead Nurturing and Profiling

When you *do* social media, it's important to target your efforts so you're doing it *right*. According to social media strategist Dustin DeTorres, while most consumer marketers immediately set up shop on Facebook and Twitter, B2B sales professionals have flocked to LinkedIn.

Designed for professional interaction, LinkedIn takes a far more sophisticated approach to networking than its social media siblings. Far beyond just posting status updates or vacation snapshots, members can disclose professional affiliations and whether or not they're open to business communication.

Of course, unsolicited LinkedIn messages work just as well as other forms of spam—*not well at all*. That's why LinkedIn members use a variety of unique, user-friendly tools to reach out to each other ethically and professionally. Members can facilitate introductions through their networks or pay for guaranteed messages to their prospects. Message recipients can choose to ignore unsolicited mail, but introductions from trusted connections tend to open online doors like they do in the real world.

LinkedIn's robust database can enhance or replace a traditional customer relationship management system. Members can view a prospect's work history, professional connections, and published books and articles. For a B2B marketer, this treasure trove of data can help target the right prospects without the frustration of cold calls or strained presentations.

LinkedIn Emphasizes Quality Leads

LinkedIn offers neutral territory for negotiation and conversation. Having been burned in the past, most professionals have become extremely protective about their contact information. Instead of watching your calls drop into a voice mail black hole, LinkedIn direct messages offer a safe way for prospects to interact with you while protecting their personal phone numbers and e-mail addresses.

LinkedIn also tracks accountability. Prospects who appreciate promptness love the ability to track responses to social media direct messages. On LinkedIn and other services, a prospect will see just how long it takes for you to respond to a request. Depending on your industry, a fast response time could mean the difference between a prospect and a sale.

Whether you delve into social media or not, don't give up maintaining your company's core website, especially if you've trained prospects to reach out to you there for sales or support requests. However, for prospects who discover you on LinkedIn or other social media networks, your responsiveness and authenticity will determine whether you'll close an eventual deal.

Search Engine Optimization versus Social Media Optimization

Over the past decade, consumer marketers have developed a host of best practices designed to drive organic search traffic. To catch the attention of buyers, marketers might

- guest post on blogs throughout an industry vertical or a community sector,
- blend traditional public relations with blog outreach campaigns designed to grow back links, or
- cultivate product and service reviews tied to affiliate programs.

Despite some recent shakeups in the way search engines calculate rankings, many ethical search engine optimization (SEO) tactics can still help B2C marketers connect the dots between a target's initial interest and an eventual purchase.

However, let's not be ignorant to the fact that the largest search engine is now a major player in the social media space. Social media is beginning to fill a void in the search engines that will soon become much more heavily relied upon in ranking algorithms. When the largest player in the world of search makes a big shift to social media, all marketers better begin to pay attention and ensure they are in the right space, in the right way.

However, as pharmaceutical industry communications expert Mark Senak points out, social media optimization should command at least as much attention as SEO in any B2B marketer's budget. Senak acknowledges that many companies have forced themselves to overcome fears about compliance and distraction on the way to an effective social media optimization (SMO) strategy.

SMO matters, now more than ever, because a growing number of professionals rely more on recommendations from peers and friends than from ten blue links on a search engine results page. Years of overoptimization have jaded some search engine power users, and they no longer trust whether the top results for a search term will offer the most reliable results or the most popular, fixed, or "rated" results. Instead, well-connected social media users post the same question on LinkedIn or Twitter that they once would have submitted to a search engine; in return, they get much better, more targeted, and more personal SMO results.

Unlike B2C marketers, who might plan for direct engagement at the heart of their SMO plans, B2B marketers can use an SMO strategy that empowers existing customers to offer testimony on their behalf, in the form of reader reviews, ratings, and more. In a cynical marketplace that expects marketers to jump at any opportunity to sell themselves, buyers often respond to genuine recommendations from satisfied clients.

Thought Leadership

With lead generation and SMO in place, B2B marketers can build a solid platform for what's known in the industry as "thought leadership." While this phrase gets tossed around far too often as a marketing buzzword, the core principle of being known as an expert at solving specific problems still holds water, particularly in the field of social media. Instead of chasing a traditional marketing funnel, a thought leadership strategy means making yourself and your brand attractive to prospects well outside the typical buying cycle. Rather than competing for attention during a request for proposals, you become the only viable candidate on your prospect's short list.

Achieving thought leadership as a B2B marketer in the industrial industry requires a generous approach to investing time in your specific, targeted audience. Executing an effective campaign means you'll send far fewer resources during an active sales process because you'll have already answered many of your prospects' questions through your content marketing over an extended period of time.

Thought leadership campaigns can include

- white papers,
- seminars,

- conferences,
- responding to questions on services like Quora and LinkedIn groups,
- guest columns in reputable industry journals, and
- published books or videos.

Strategy consultant Dorie Clark emphasizes that thought leadership requires a distinct association with quality. Connections with traditional media, such as a guest column in a respected industry periodical or a guest posting on a respected industry blog, show prospects that your claims have been vetted by journalists and critics. In an environment where anyone can publish anything, true thought leaders share ideas that hold up under scrutiny and intense peer review.

Brand Reinforcement

Thought leadership contributes to the maintenance or the revitalization of your brand. B2C marketers sometimes lean too heavily on display advertising and gimmicks that seek to establish a presence—oftentimes at any cost—to make an impression.

For B2B marketers, an online presence isn't enough to close a deal—especially when everyone and their brother is online as well. Instead, strong brand reinforcement builds on the profiling, SMO, and thought leadership campaign you've developed in the early stages of your social media strategy.

Brand reinforcement can occur after your initial interaction or even your initial sale. You're most vulnerable during this downtime in a client's buying cycle. Competitors can use the same thought leadership strategies to insert themselves into the top of your customers' minds, throwing roadblocks in the way of repeat or expanded business.

Instead, keep your customers warm when they're not directly in need of your services. Use the same strategies that won their business in the first place, while emphasizing a high level of care and support after your sale. This closes out the sales loop in a way that keeps them in your circle of care as long as they're fed and watered with quality follow-through and service.

Forbes contributor Michael Matthews points out that brand reinforcement doesn't mean giving up on sales. In fact, you should be using those repeated touch points with customers as *opportunities to sell*. Placing value on a seminar or an event, even when you announce that you're donating proceeds to charity, keeps your prospects accustomed to the premium nature of your products and services regardless of the event or premium you're offering.

A Case Study in Quality

Are you having difficulty translating your material product into the digital world? Are you overwhelmed by implementing successful social media strategies into your marketing plan?

If you are having a hard time making Internet-based media work for your company, you probably have a lot of questions about ways to better yourself. For a good example of how social media is done right, take a look at what Sharpie has been doing with their digital campaigns to make the most of their presence on the web. By following some of these techniques, you can make yourself more relevant in the changing digital world and make social media worth your while.

Sharp as a Tack: A Case Study in Sharpie

With a tagline like "Uncap what's inside," you know that Sharpie means to leave an impression whether they're marketing online or off. Founded in 1964, Sharpie has long been the first name of the marker world. How do they translate their traditional product for the tangible world to the modern digital world of technology?

The answer can be found in interactive social media:

- **Facebook:** With over 3.6 million page "likes" and counting, Sharpie is no fool when it comes to Facebook. Their page features a hand-drawn cover photo on their timeline, daily updates, seamlessly intertwined user content, surveys, videos, contests, and more. Content from other Sharpie media outlets is incorporated through their Facebook feed, as well. Sharpie also "likes" relevant pages, such as Office Depot, Target, DIY Movement, and more, spreading the love to retailers and users.
- **Twitter:** While still relatively new, Sharpie's Twitter page boasts just over 236,000 followers. Daily updates, including information about what's going on at the Sharpie website, an Instagram album featuring user photos of Sharpies in action, and frequent interactions with followers makes Sharpie's Twitter account a hit with fans.
- **YouTube:** Sharpie's YouTube channel, SharpieUS, has nearly 1,700 subscribers and well over 1.3 million video views. They've smartly divided categories of video—such as Get Inspired, How to Draw, and Sharpie Squad—into various playlists to make them more relevant for the user's interests. Celebrity endorsements are sprinkled throughout, catching the eye of people who would otherwise not intend to seek out the Sharpie channel.
- **Sharpie.com:** The Sharpie website showcases all the product lines, and it has many elements that connect to other social media accounts. The Sharpie blog is frequently updated with photos, videos, and links to contests and more. It also features posts from guest bloggers and the Sharpie Squad, a small group of fans and artists chosen annually to represent Sharpie and to test new products while cross-promoting. MySharpie.com is a micro-site for users to upload, connect, and share with other Sharpie enthusiasts.

Leaving Your Own Mark

Sharpie very successfully uses social media to tell a story. Rather than putting their advertising focus on *who* they are, they showcase *what* they are—a tool for telling a creative story. As the tagline indicates, it's what's inside that matters—not the name on the side. How can you utilize Sharpie's success in social media to make your own mark on the web?

Follow these tips to get your business on the right track:

- **Put the emphasis on the customer.** Interact with your fans to let them tell your story for you.
- **Update all forms of media frequently.** Keeping content fresh keeps it relevant and in the eyes of those who you want to see it.
- **Change the focus from you to them.** As shown with Sharpie, your users are your most viable spokespeople.
- **Use Facebook and Twitter updates as opportunities to ask questions of your consumers and as a way to start a conversation with them.** These portals are always open and work both ways.
- **Include interactive tools, such as surveys and contests, on your Facebook page.**

  o What's your favorite thing about our product/service?

  o How could we improve our products/services?

  o Have you found any unconventional ways for using our product/service?

  o What is your favorite thing about our company?

- **Directly reply to tweets from Twitter followers—engage with them often.** The difference between followers who tweet you once and those who tweet you regularly, usually depends on how often you respond to them. Not responding to active engagement is a missed opportunity.

- Cross-reference your social media outlets to build a network across platforms and incorporate one medium into another. Use who follows you on Twitter, for instance, to recommend who to invite to like you on Facebook. Set up your tweets to appear on Facebook and your Facebook posts to appear on Twitter. Refer Facebook fans to your Twitter page, send Twitter fans to look at new YouTube videos, and post YouTube videos to your wall on Facebook.

By implementing some of Sharpie's strategies into your marketing plan, you too can have success in social media. It just takes a little ingenuity and creativity on your part. Are you ready to write your digital legacy? What will you do first?

Online Videos: How and Why They Would be Effective in Marketing Your Industry

Increasingly, viewers aren't just getting their entertainment through online videos, but their news, information and consumer education as well. The use of online videos is arguably one of the most transcendent and effective marketing strategies today. Many large companies and industries are increasingly investing a lot of money in creating and promoting themselves via this method. In fact, the CNNMoney report on online videos has stated that in the past year, online videos attracted the majority of the consumer traffic for the first time (53 percent).

That fact obviously qualifies online videos as a solid and reliable marketing method, particularly in light of the fact that now we can view these online videos anywhere we go: on our cell phones, tablets, Kindles, Nooks, etc. It should come as no surprise that, by 2015, it is expected that more than 66 percent of the Internet will be comprised of videos. What makes online videos such an attraction? How can you strategize and invest in them? And is the investment really worth it?

A significant percentage of online businesses or industries are only relying on content marketing, banners, link building, etc. Although these methods may be effective, depending on how they are implemented, more creativity is required in the field of marketing. Marketers perfectly understand that the most effectual marketing methods are the ones that consumers can easily relate to.

We live in a largely video-oriented society. Even basic forms of entertainment come in video form. Most people have grown up engrossed by television screens and computers for motion picture entertainment. Additionally, they use the Internet mostly for video viewing and sharing. In fact, YouTube attracts more than sixty hours of video upload every minute—and more than 3 billion video views per day. Therefore, you can easily connect and relate with such a target market through online videos.

Online videos form a sturdier marketing platform than other online marketing methods. A 2010 survey by *Forbes* revealed that more than 60 percent of the general website traffic watches videos even before reading the web page content. Another 22 percent confirmed that they prefer watching videos to reading business reviews.

The use of online videos may seem like an easily implementable marketing strategy. However, there is stiff competition with this marketing option since the Internet has billions of videos. To make your videos stand out among the rest, there are crucial factors that you ought to consider as you shoot, edit, and upload your marketing videos:

- **Always use a Tripod.** Bare hands are not firm enough to shoot a high-quality video without shaking.
- **Your video, regardless of its simplicity, must be accompanied by audio.** This may be in form of music, sound effects, or conversation.
- **Regardless of a video's simplicity, it must be shot and edited by professionals.** Few things are as

counterproductive as spending time, energy, creativity, and resources on a video that, once posted, does more harm than good by eroding the brand because it looks like it was produced by amateurs.

- **The lighting of a video clip is the most crucial quality-determining factor.** Therefore, your videos have to be shot under sufficient lighting.

To excellently promote your videos to the target market, you have to:

- **Prepare a solid video promotional plan.** Don't just get infatuated with the process of making videos; know, going in, how they're going to be used as an integral part of your marketing plan. Video marketing is different than print or other forms of marketing, and you must do a little work to find out the best way to promote them.
- **Define the target market, clients, and directories—and promote your videos to them.** Just as with any other form of marketing, you have to get the right people interested. To do so, know who your target audience is, produce videos they'd be interested in watching, and then funnel them toward those videos.
- **Optimize your videos for easy keyword detection via search engines.** Have distinct titles, make them easy to find, and link them if possible by numbers in a series (see below).
- **Brand all your videos.** Your videos won't effectively promote your business if they are not ideally branded with logos, trademarks, etc.
- **Connect your videos.** Rather than just randomly posting an assortment of videos, connect them by doing several series of videos that all link to each other, or continue on from last week's video, or are numbered, like "six tips" or "five secrets," etc. These get users to watch more than one video and entice them to subscribe to your channel to

get additional videos in the series without having to hunt them down.

Online video marketing may be an exceptional strategy, but its effectiveness and overall results are dependent upon how you implement it. Therefore, as you embrace this marketing method, you have to be creative to ensure that you are always one step ahead of your competitors.

Why should your business concentrate on minimally effective marketing strategies when you can use videos to effectively and conveniently reach out to the market?

LinkedIn and Google Plus Are the Most Advantageous for Industrial and B2B Companies

There are so many social media outlets to choose from—from LinkedIn to Facebook, from Twitter to Pinterest, Klout to Foursquare. Which ones to choose? How much time to spend on each? For my money, two major networks can have an immediate impact for B2B companies.

LinkedIn

If you don't have a LinkedIn account, what are you waiting for? With more than 175 million members (as of this writing), LinkedIn is the largest and fastest-growing professional network on the Internet.

Social networking sites can be confusing and easy to misuse if you don't know all the ins and outs. They're often complicated with more features than meet the eye; even if you think you know what you are doing, you may be missing some vital features. What can you do to get the most out of your LinkedIn account? Let's discuss some basic steps for getting started that you can implement to more effectively build your professional network—resulting in more contacts and more business.

Linking In (So You Don't Miss Out!)

Basic LinkedIn accounts are free to create and easy to set up. You can start on the site's main page to join and follow the prompts (http://www.linkedin.com/). Once you've created an account, here's how to make the most of your profile:

- **Add a photo.** A user profile is what makes you a real, tangible person to people viewing your profile. Do not skip this step. Choose a professional-looking photo, even if it is not a proper headshot.
- **Import your resume.** If you're looking for an easy button, this is it. LinkedIn has a feature that allows you to import your resume, and it auto-fills many of your fields for you.
- **Beef it up.** Don't stop after importing your resume. Personalize! Your profile is more than a resume—it's an extension of you. Breathe your life into it. Let it tell your story for you.
- **Add personal interests, such as cycling, running, or painting.** Be more than a picture and a paragraph; become personal to those who seek out your profile.
- **Don't be afraid to brag where appropriate.** Discuss awards, recognition, certifications, and qualifications in detail.
- **Experience and education count.** Be sure to talk about your education and experiences in school.
- **Always be SEO-ing.** Your profile is searchable by keyword; include a wide range of vocabulary to describe your interests and experiences.

Also, remember that your profile will be compared to those of your competitors, so make it look the best you can. Here's how:

- **Get connected.** The power of LinkedIn is in your network. Find former and current colleagues, classmates, people with whom you've done business, and friends, and request to connect with them. You want to build the widest network possible; try not to leave anyone out.

- **Recommendations.** This is the equivalent of the references section of your resume. It's also what can separate a good profile from a great one. Don't be too shy to ask for recommendations from your connections; likewise, be sure to return the favor. When you are getting started, it is often easier to give recommendations before asking for them.

- **Join groups.** Groups are a great way to expand your network, make more connections, and meet more people. To start, join like-minded groups, such as alumni, chambers, and hobby groups, as well as industry-specific local, regional, and national groups. Groups are your ticket to expanding your network quickly and efficiently. Use them to demonstrate expertise in your industry by offering solutions to posted questions—and as a tool to educate yourself.

- **Status updates.** Update your status daily to keep your name appearing on the feed of your connections, but don't overwhelm them with too many updates. Keep your updates business-related, and use them to post questions, conduct polls, talk about upcoming and recent events, and discuss employment opportunities.

Arming yourself with these basic tools will allow you to make the most of your LinkedIn account and use it rather than just post it. Yes, it can be work, but taking the time to build the best profile possible from the start will save you time and effort in the long run—and helps effortlessly expand your network and build your business contacts exponentially. Ensure that you have a strong link (profile), so you can build an even stronger chain (network).

Google Plus: Using Google Plus to boost your brand's recognition

A great resource for understanding how to use Google Plus is through Chris Brogan's *Google Plus for Business: How Google's Social Network Changes Everything* (Que Publishing, 2011). Brogan espouses what many of us have already learned: Google Plus has gained over one hundred million users in the year since its launch. When the search engine that controls your website's fate puts out a social network, marketers better pay attention.

It reached forty million users and one hundred million users faster than any other social media site, including Twitter and Facebook. Most companies are contemplating whether they need another social network brand page. The basic answer is yes, but the longer, stronger answer is *Google Plus takes the social search to a whole new level.*

For those readers who still doubt the power of this revolution in global social media, here is a relatively easy way to demonstrate the power of Google Plus in search results:

- Log in to your Google Plus account.
- Search for a company on Google that you have not followed on Google Plus.
- Follow the company on Google Plus.
- Search for the company or brand after following it on Google Plus.

Almost always, the company jumps several positions in the search results, depending on the brand's activity on Google Plus. The search results also indicate how many people follow the company's page. Most users tend to visit pages with more followers since this acts as a form of silent endorsement by other people.

You need to register and set up a brand page before using Google Plus. Follow these steps to register:

- Set up a Gmail address for your business.
- Visit Create a Page and follow the instructions.
- Choose the category your business.
- Make sure all fields are filled and then fully customize the profile page.
- Start using your Google Plus brand page.

The most common pitfall in most brand pages is poor setup. This is mainly manifested by poorly filled details and inaccurate information. For a brand page to be effective as a marketing tool, it has to be set up well and have a large enough following.

Get a Targeted Following With Google Plus

Connections are the commerce of social media; in that regard, Google Plus is no different. Therefore, the easiest way to garner a vast following on Google Plus is by leveraging your current following on other social networks. This is done by sharing the link to your Google Plus profile on these sites. Another way is to have a profile badge on your company website and other online avenues featuring your content, where the Google Plus affiliation is both visible and easily followed.

Google Plus provided many simple ways to utilize its features for all users.

Circles

One feature unique to Google Plus, which is invaluable for brand management, is the circles feature. Different circles should be set up for various customer groups. This will help in interacting with various groups separately. If, for example, a new service for medical professionals is being unveiled, the company will communicate the release only to medical professionals via a message to all members of this circle.

Hangouts

The hangouts features can be used in several ways, depending on the need. A company can use live video conferencing in hangouts as a live support feature. This will provide true interaction in case of physical problems since the support assistant can see what the problem is and can give relevant directions.

The hangouts feature can also be used to host live discussions between customers and company representatives. The hangout on air feature allows broadcast of a hangout to an unlimited audience like an interactive live TV broadcast.

The best way to effectively use the hangout on air feature would be setting up a broadcast schedule. A schedule informs your customer base when the next hangout will be. This will allow all interested customers to tune in and chat. Hangout on air can be used as a Q&A session or a product launch. Customers can make suggestions in areas where products can be improved during these hangouts.

Google Live Events

When holding a live event, you should register it with www.googleliveevents.com. By registering a live event on the Google live events, you can attract followers who are not in your circles to tune in and watch. In the long run, this will increase your brand visibility and your amount of followers, which is one of the main reasons for using social media.

Case Study: Sony Uses Google Plus to Strengthen Their Brand

One great example of a company using Google Plus effectively to strengthen its brand is Sony. On its Google Plus page, Sony has set up thirteen different circles for various products, such as PlayStation, Sony Pictures, and Sony Xperia.

Sony also holds regular hangouts in which it gives its followers the scoop on various products and upcoming events. Sony has integrated the hangout feature with its YouTube channel. By integrating hangouts with YouTube, followers can watch recorded hangouts from a company's YouTube channel.

As Sony and many other companies can attest, Google Plus is taking the social search experience to a new level. Have you tried Google Plus today?

Measuring the ROI of Social Media

So, is this all worth it? The profile pictures and links and networks and tweets? It's exciting and fun and lends itself to creativity, but can we monetize it?

The industrial marketing process doesn't exactly lend itself to decision making without company-to-client discussions, negotiations, and detailed analysis. Given this fact, a number of B2B managers are wondering if it's necessary to use social media to a great degree. Since they aren't attracting consumers who can make a buying decision based on a connection they made, social media tends not to take on a great urgency with industrial managers.

However, this lack of urgency is due to the lack of clear connection between the leads at the top of the marketing funnel and direct social media activity. If there was a clear and measurable indication that social media drew prospects toward the company, its use would call for more intentional involvement. Moreover, if that measurement was specific enough to provide data about which social networks were the most productive, then focusing personnel on them would be a priority.

A definitive science on ROI for social media has not yet been widely accepted. Calculations range from the extremely complex measurement of all possible inputs to the simplicity of basic outcomes of leads and prospects. The discussion is likely to remain fluid given the focus in 2011 on social media activity's effects on Google search rankings. Depending on how dependent a company's lead generation funnel is on Google, it is possible that its social media involvement could have little direct influence on lead generation—but a significant influence on search rankings.

However, companies can track and measure specific input and outputs to develop a sense of how social media adds to their marketing funnel. On the input side, companies should be measuring its costs in terms of the amount of staff time being spent to undertake engagement across the networks. These costs should offset or be offset by cost savings that come from reduced spending on traditional media advertising.

With respect to outputs, companies should track two specific criteria:

1. Where do leads come into the marketing system?
2. How many of the leads are the result of social media activity?

Given that a company has the ability to segment its tracking systems, focus should be placed on *how many of these leads convert to buying discussions*. Because of the nature of an industrial sales cycle and its focus on relationship building, marketers should learn from customers how they became interested in a particular product or service.

However, structure is needed to scale this process to fit both large and small industrial companies.

- Companies should carefully construct, tag, and segment tracking systems so they know where leads are coming into their system down to the level of individual social media platform. This could mean setting up different opt-in processes for each network a company uses to engage the public.

- Companies should carefully track their investment in human capital to the social media process. Whether a company chooses to aggregate salary dollars or use a man-hours concept, an attempt should be made to keep tabs on how much is being spent specifically on engagement.
- Companies that use social media in lieu of branding expenses of any kind should intelligently add this component into ROI calculations.
- Companies must know their points of conversion. At what point in the process do prospects move to buying conversations. Executives must be adept at knowing and notating the source of these conversions.
- Companies can calculate basic measurements by taking into account

  o which leads came to the system through social media channels,
  o how much those leads tend to be worth in profit contribution,
  o how many of the leads actually converted to customer conversations, and
  o what the social media leads specifically brought to the company in the way of revenue and profit.

The concept of calculating the ROI of social media will shift when there are changes in how the platforms structure their networks. Additionally, as businesses grow in their use of these platforms, more robust marketing measurement models will be developed that will benefit companies of all sizes.

As companies grow more comfortable with measuring social media's ROI, will they increase their investment of time and resources? The ROI of social media will prove itself out and quickly become a dependable and reliable stream that few B2B companies can do without.

CHAPTER 11

From White Paper to Webinar— Technical Content

There is a marked creative difference in creating casual or trade market content, such as general interest blog posts or even "light" brochure copy, and writing what we all know as "technical" content that is more B2B and industry-relatable.

In this chapter we'll focus in on two critical pieces of technical content—white papers and webinars—that will help take your technical marketing to the next level in the critical B2B market.

Creating Effective White Papers

There are many tools a company has in its arsenal to state its case to prospective customers, but the white paper can be the most potent when it is used effectively. Essentially, a white paper is content that easily makes the transition from the web to physical handout while retaining its effect in the marketplace.

Most importantly, the format communicates a seriousness about the brand and/or the product that an online article, video, or image cannot do as easily. Because the white paper is a well-researched and factual presentation of your company's assessment of how to solve a real-life business problem, the document is considered a more trustworthy marketing piece than a standard brochure or a presentation.

Additionally, since it is expected to have a certain length, you can go into detail about topics, discussions, and solutions in a way that isn't readily available to you in a one-page blog post or simple catalog copy.

What Is a White Paper—and Why Is It Trusted?

Far from a creative document, the white paper originated in government as a way for proposals to be made to start new projects, request funding, and consider new legislation.

Because of this requirement, the structure of the communication needed to be objective, with critical and analytical depth that indicated that sufficient research had been done to cover all contingencies. Because the form was so effective at selling new ideas and concepts, it eventually evolved into a marketing tool.

The Evolution of the White Paper

White papers are used by companies to educate prospects and clients as well as the general public on what is required to solve certain problems. For that reason, they have evolved into a quasi-document that is academic *and* promotional.

The research involved in assessing solutions is also used by successful companies to boost their image and brand in a new or experimental niche. Moreover, white papers are now used to position companies as thought leaders in mitigating the effects of new problems that don't have commonly known and practiced solutions.

This makes it even more critical for you to see the difference and value in a white paper as opposed to other, less serious marketing content. When done right, a carefully crafted and particularly useful white paper can set you and your company in an entirely different light.

A Good White Paper Educates to Sell

Any good white paper brings the knowledge of the prospect or client up a notch about the depth and impact of a particular problem. Its focus should be, first and foremost, on education versus selling.

In some cases, this part of the education process is critical because those to whom you are presenting may not know or understand how a particular issue is affecting them or their marketplace.

The objective presentation of the problem and the negative consequences of allowing it to go unresolved can influence those who make purchase commitments. It is also a mitigating factor for many who will openly share and distribute a quality, impartial, and objective white paper, hence expanding your reach and reputation, versus shutting down one that is clearly intended "just" to sell.

White Paper Topics Solve Problems

When a company decides to seriously commit to writing a white paper, it should consider the most confounding problems in its industry. Typically these problems are going to revolve around things that affect costs and/or revenues, such as automation, quality control, and systems upgrades.

However, the problem being analyzed could also have a more indirect linkage to costs and revenues, such as employee morale or shipping solutions. Regardless of the topic being discussed, it should be one that a prospect has a need or desire to resolve as soon as possible.

How Long Should a Good White Paper Be?

The way to approach this piece of research is not to work toward a predetermined length that is set in stone. There is no "magic bullet" length where people will stop reading if it's longer or be disappointed if it's shorter.

The most important issue is that it flows to the right amount of depth in communicating the nature and effect of the problem. Many confuse a white paper with an executive summary, but you don't want to promise big results without delivering a thorough analysis of the problem as well as a realistic solution. Because every niche is different and the nature of its problems is diverse, it is difficult to determine the proper amount of content in a white paper.

The question that every company should ask before completing the process shouldn't be centered around how long it is, but about what it takes to achieve the educational goal. Here are some good discussion questions to help you arrive at that answer:

- Is the prospect or customer aware of the depth of the issue you are writing about?
- Do they recognize what not solving the problem could mean to their revenues and/or costs?
- Are they calculating any potential strain that the issue could be placing on their human resources?

The educational process needs to be long enough for the reader to have credible and reliable information to make a good purchase decisions.

The Four-Part Structure of the White Paper

The structure of a good white paper is very basic, but the critical factor is that each stage should engage and prepare the buyer for a soft sales pitch at the end.

1.) **Introduction:** A short section designed to inform readers of the problem you'll be discussing, why it's relevant to your industry, and how you'll solve it.

2.) **Discussion of the problem:** A thorough, in-depth, analytical discussion of the problem that goes as deep as necessary.

3.) **Nature of the solution:** A general and broad discussion about the solution or solutions to the problem being discussed.

4.) **Conclusion or sales pitch:** How your company can help the client provide a solution.

Although the tone of a white paper should be serious and detailed, that doesn't meant it should in any way, shape, or form be ponderous to read or intimidating to look at. The appearance of the white paper should be very easy to read—with graphics and photos to make the information clear. Although a call to action is necessary, the text should be void of a sales pitch until the conclusion. A white paper is a soft-sell piece, heavy on the education, not a hard sell letter.

At its heart, the document is a well-researched proof piece about the depth of your understanding of a prospect's market and what a solution can actually do for them. While the time spent researching, crafting, and publishing a white paper can be considerable, so are the payoffs.

Because a completed white paper has, inherent in it, significant resources in research and writing, a company should repurpose the content many times. While it should naturally be posted to the company's web properties, it should also be viewed as worthy to be recontextualized in local, regional, and national trade publications. Moreover, the content can also be used in e-mail/e-courses, press releases, and high-level sales presentations to senior executives.

To make this document inherently more shareable, be mindful of these properties during the creation phase. Look for quotable moments to repurpose in shorter form, excerpts, or statistics that could be used as lead-ins for press releases and the like. Make it easy for others to use this information by having various lengths available.

A white paper states to the marketplace that you are a leader and problem solver. Good marketing messages communicate your unique position in the marketplace. That message can be made superior with proof that a company understands its prospects' needs and constraints—and that is where the white paper format truly shines.

At What Point Do You Measure the ROI on Content Marketing?

Regardless of what type of marketing you're doing, every business needs to evaluate whether the money they are spending brings profits. Does it make sense to continue spending money if you cannot prove that it works?

If you're spending staff time or company resources to have content created, particularly time- and personnel-extensive content like white papers, you may not see customers come streaming through your doors the next day. However, there should be a time when you can point to the positive and quantifiable results of your content marketing to say that it works.

It is a marketing industry maxim that the more you spend on the content, the higher the quality you'll get as a result. But an equally universal question asks if that higher quality translates into higher profits.

Content Marketing

As we have seen throughout this book, companies can use multiple forms of content to market their business effectively. It's critical to determine which content belongs in which format—for which market. In some cases, an article is the most appropriate tool; in other cases, a video or podcast may be the most convincing. Still, in other scenarios, a company can use a more connected form of communication on a blog or social media platform. All mediums are necessary if a company wants to be successful in meeting their prospect on their (the prospect's) terms.

What Content Marketing *Should* Do

In terms of composition, each of these content forms—social entries, videos, articles, or podcasts—require about the same level of intensity to make them effective marketing tools.

While they need to be factual, they also imagine the potential benefits—and state them as facts. These kinds of content pieces aren't meant to be objective. They are meant to move prospects into a marketing funnel to become buyers.

Keeping Content Marketing Cost Effective: Repurposing Content

For the most part, a savvy business owner can repurpose content for each medium so that it is specific and well received. It wouldn't take much effort or many resources to retrofit an article into the subject of a video or podcast. In essence, the article could become the script for such content. The same would be true of turning it into a press release or infographic for sharing on social media.

The basic inputs for each of these media are interchangeable. In fact, many business owners are skilled at republishing content within available forms. They are, at their core, article-based content delivered over a variety of mediums.

For instance, a solid, well-written general interest magazine article-length piece could be repurposed in a variety of ways:

- several blog posts
- a full-length podcast

- two or three shorter podcasts
- video blogs or webinars on the topic
- quotable talking points for a press release

White Papers Should Be Treated Differently

When a business decides to have white paper content created, the formulas are somewhat different. The purpose of a white paper is to present objective research as the foundation for problem solving and good decision making. It positions the creator as an expert on the problems being discussed and solved within the content, but its goal is not to wrestle a customer through a sales pitch camouflaged as usable data.

The research in a white paper is typically more sophisticated, even targeted, than the background for article-based content. It is composed of industry reports, studies, interviews, and even university-based consultation. Getting the research right is more of a priority than forcing it into the professional straitjacket of a favorable conclusion.

The white paper's primary sales tactic is to present the company and/or its management as experts in articulating the problems of a particular industry in an objective, useful, compelling way.

When a company is successful in preserving the integrity of the research, its management can position its researchers and decision makers as experts in the industry. How can a company leverage this research for additional revenues?

Repurposing White Paper Content: Private Webinars

One effective sales tool that a company can use to repurpose creative content across another platform is a webinar. The webinar allows a company to present its white paper findings to concerned professionals all over the world—without the expense and constraints of an industry conference. A webinar can be the perfect format to present the research in a straightforward manner—while allowing for feedback and questions.

Presenting research and discussing conclusions is likely to take longer than the average length of an Internet video or podcast. It also does not lend itself well to the short, readable conclusions that are needed to keep an article readable. Presenting the data on a webinar, when attendees' expectations are to be able to focus for forty-five minutes to an hour, can bridge the gap that other content forms cannot do effectively.

Additionally, the registration process of a webinar allows a company to collect the contact information of interested attendees. The contact information of prospects who are interested in the solution to the problem promoted for the webinar is an *extremely* powerful set of data.

Management will not have to guess how to be effective in marketing messages to those attendees. The chief benefit of doing a webinar presentation instead of waiting for a conference or industry seminar is control over the targeted prospect list. Imagine how long it would take to amass such a list in a piecemeal, one-on-one gathering process.

Ten Steps to Repurposing White Paper Content

Here are the ten simple steps a company needs to take in order to repurpose high-quality content in a webinar or teleseminar for maximum benefit:

1. **Summarize the most important points of the white paper's research.** A summary provides added value in that it highlights key points for busy readers on the go, and it lays out your case by strategically expressing the quality content contained in the paper itself.
2. **Identify and define each of the important points according to documented problems in the industry.**

This documentation can come from the news, trade journals, magazines, conference findings, social media, and Internet searches.

3. **Create presentations based on documented industry problems as the title or subject of the presentation.** Although neither the basic content nor conclusions from the white paper should change, the basis for discussing it is adaptable.

4. **Prioritize industry problems according to those of interest to the widest range of industry professionals.** Although it is not a trade publication meant for mass consumption, your white paper should be easily consumable—and attractive—far and wide to those in your industry.

5. **Starting with the first documented problem, create content meant to attract readers, listeners, and viewers from different online and offline mediums.** The end of each presentation should include a way to learn more, which will be the registration link for your webinar or webinar series.

6. **Keep the end results—marketing and closing prospects—in mind.** The preparation of the prewebinar process should include a method for collecting contact information and a way to deliver more content on the subject.

7. **Close with confidence.** The preparation of the post-webinar process should include a procedure for following up with prospects and targeted messaging based on the webinar's subject matter.

8. **Promote the webinar using SEO, podcasting, video marketing, social media, public relations, trade journal articles, conference appearances, guest blogging, etc.** Promote the webinar as defined by the problem—not the white paper or the actual solution.

9. **Any presentation of the company's products or services should be soft-sold.** Conduct the webinar

in a way that shows you understand the depth of the problem—and what allowing the issue to go unmitigated would mean.

10. **Apply as necessary.** In order to make white paper and webinar marketing a habitual rather than one-time behavior, repeat the process according to your prioritized list of documented problems.

Seven Steps for Turning Technical Content to Tactical Marketing

Research can be a powerful marketing tool when used in concert with types of online or offline media that lend themselves to its presentation. Webinars should be used liberally to attract prospects into a company's marketing funnel. Taking an active role in the content process in this way can increase the ROI of content marketing.

Research published in the *Harvard Business Review* suggests that traditional solution selling has lost traction to a new kind of B2B approach. Star sales performers must identify prospects who already know about products and solutions—but need to cope quickly with change. To tap into this rapidly evolving online marketplace, use these seven steps to position your company as a trusted partner to survive that disruption:

Step 1: *Profile your audience.*

Create B2B content that appeals to your prospects, while filtering out tire-kickers and readers outside your target market. Discover the minimum number of posts you'll need each month to be effective, something that author Michael Hyatt says that many bloggers "overestimate."

In many cases, less really is more, particularly if you're taking Step 1 to heart and targeting a specific audience. Focus on just one or two niches that you can dominate, instead of spreading your appeal too thin for little or no results.

Step 2: *Set editorial standards.*

Additional research into social media strategies from the *Harvard Business Review* identified four specific ways to supercharge your B2B blog posts and status updates:

1.) **Challenge your audience to think differently about a topic.** You can disrupt your prospects' world view even further by fanning the right flames and creating impactful statements that encourage readers to hear more from you.
2.) **Share relevant insights and details about your audience's needs.** Explore how you can help them thrive in a changing market—and do it in a way that is unique to you. Don't follow the same path as everyone else.
3.) **Ask relevant questions about your audience.** You'll foster discussion while identifying potential leads and connecting in real and insightful ways.
4.) **Ask for the sale.** Research indicates that B2B readers respect an occasional event invitation or product announcement. Don't overlook them as part of the natural and organic promotional process.

As Bob Apollo points out, you'll clutter your blog and your social media streams with too many "off-topic" posts, "good morning" wishes, or other noisy content. Find out what you do best, who needs it the most, and drill down as deeply as you can into these two corridors.

Step 3: *Prepare your annual editorial calendar.*

Many of you may be saying to yourself, "An editorial *what?* Am I running a magazine now?" However, a well-planned editorial calendar can take the guesswork and procrastination out of carefully crafted versus randomly chaotic social media programs. Darren Rowse of ProBlogger.net notes that something as simple as a spreadsheet lets you easily focus on weekly rhythms that carry key themes throughout the year.

With your editorial calendar in place, you no longer need to scramble for post ideas at the last minute. Instead, you can cycle through the four types of posts mentioned above, layering in a second level of hot keywords for maximum affect. Infopreneur Alan Petersen posted a downloadable Excel template you can use to map your own topics and post types.

Step 4: *Get employees to help build your content library.*

Your competitors' websites may lack personality because they follow a paint-by-numbers template. Shining the spotlight on your team shows that real, trustworthy people work at your organization—and that you recognize them as valuable assets of your company.

Assign topics from your editorial calendar far in advance, so you'll have time to edit and optimize employee content. You may even discover a few team members with hidden talents who can take over some of this work for you or become star writers.

Step 5: *Generate content from customer feedback and surveys.*

Another way to personalize your postings and make them even more pertinent to your audience is to give your audience a voice. Every time a customer calls with a question about your product or service or leaves feedback at your website, online catalog, or blog, capture that interaction as a potential source for B2B content. Scheduling posts based on customer concerns eliminates frustration from prospects with too little patience to pick up the phone.

Step 6: *Interview peers, partners, and thought leaders.*

Your B2B content gives you the power to stage your own version of an industry convention every day. Invite guest authors to contribute to your library, especially when you serve overlapping audiences. Quick interviews and Q&A sessions can generate easy content, especially if you post transcripts of your conversations.

Step 7: *Repurpose your content for complementary platforms.*

With a little effort, you can convert your best writing into other formats that can travel with your prospects:

- **White papers.** Format your best blog posts as PDF reports that your prospects can print out and share among their own teams.
- **Newsletters.** Your audience won't check your site every day, but you can bring them up to speed with a weekly e-mail. You'll build a permission asset with measurable results.
- **Webinars.** Some of your prospects prefer to interact with people during real-time presentations. Let your audience tune in to conferences or hangouts where you discuss your recent posts.
- **Podcasts.** Inexpensive tools let you record insightful, FM-quality conversations with your team, your customers, and other thought leaders.
- **Videos.** Record your in-house presentations for YouTube and podcasting platforms.

Scheduling additional blog posts to announce the release of these alternate formats is a great excuse to revisit your "best of" material, while still faithfully following your editorial calendar. Revisit all seven steps a few times each year—and adjust your course based on your results.

Parting Words

White papers and webinars are two forms of industry-specific marketing that can appeal greatly to your industrial marketing audience. The key is to know what audience you are attempting to target with each distinct form of content and to channel it in the right direction.

CHAPTER 12

Building a Customer-Driven Sales Cycle

To stay current and competitive, today's industrial businesses must use various kinds of online content—from news releases and ads to product demos, catalogs, and case studies—in order to influence potential customers.

The primary challenge nowadays is that today's savvy, sophisticated consumers will seek out various types of online content, depending on what stage of the industrial buying cycle they are in. How do you meet your customers where they are—online and during the various stages of the industrial buying cycle?

This chapter will help you build a customer-driven sales cycle that is both content- and Internet-driven. To create an effective, comprehensive strategy of online marketing, industrial marketing specialists need to understand the five stages of the buying cycle and the different forms of online content that are meaningful and valuable to buyers/consumers in each stage of the industrial buying cycle

The Five Stages of the Industrial Buying Cycle

While the Internet has made selling and buying industrial products easier, it is by no means a "point-and-click" silver bullet from the seller's perspective. B2B consumers still go through the various stages of the industrial buying cycle as they determine what's best for them.

Fortunately, their progress remains fairly predictable since the industrial buying cycle (all business-to-business buying cycles) comes with five stages:

The First Stage: Before Awareness

At this stage, the consumer is not aware that they need something or someone. Regardless, it's still possible for industrial marketers to reach and influence consumer. This way, when they do need someone or something, your business will come to mind first.

This is where having a solid, helpful, friendly brand comes in handy. Even when a marketing or promotional effort isn't immediately paying off in point-and-click purchasing, it still adds value to this particular part of the buying cycle.

The Second Stage: Awareness

During the second stage of the industrial buying cycle, the buyer/consumer realizes there's a need for a service or a product. As a result, they become more aware of providers that can solve their problems or serve their needs.

Any research that occurs during this phase is preliminary. Some online content is more effective or influential early, in the middle, or late in this stage, and we will address which ones are most appropriate for which stage in a later section of this chapter.

The Third Stage: Search for Suppliers

Nowadays, buyers are researching, investigating, and analyzing the capabilities of a company's services or products to meet a need. Regardless of how visible and effective your company may be online, a manufacturer being considered at this stage is still most likely to receive a phone call at some point throughout this phase. Similar to the second stage, there are early, middle, and late sub-phases, during which some online content is more influential.

The Fourth Stage: Settle Price and Select Vendor

During the fourth stage of the industrial buying cycle, the buyer narrows his or her choices to a select few providers. If the content needs of the buyer have been satisfied, he or she will certainly send a Request for Quotation (RFQ) or give you a phone call during this critical stage.

However, if you haven't thoroughly met their needs, your odds of being contacted are much lower. This stage is essential for promoting action from prospective buyers.

The Fifth Stage: After the Sale

Many companies only consider the first four stages of the cycle, refusing to consider a fifth. However, even after completing the transaction, online content can still be utilized to influence the consumer and increase the chance of future purchases. This is a great way to foster repeat business, referral business, etc.

Using Online Content to Influence Buyers during the Buying Cycle

Online content plays a major part in steering potential customers to your door, and it is critical during each of the five stages of the industrial buying cycle. Which type is most effective—and at which stage? You need to consider various types of online content in each stage to influence buyers successfully.

In the before awareness stage, for instance, you may use news releases and online display advertising. However, many industrial companies are starting to use social media at this phase. You might want to take advantage of that additional avenue as well.

In terms of content at this stage, be sure to include informative, quick videos about your business, news releases, and e-newsletters since these are the most interesting during the awareness stage.

By the middle and late stages of the industrial buying cycle, however, keep in mind that buyers/consumers will look for more sophisticated sources, such as a comprehensive product catalog that includes detailed and specific technical information.

A recent survey of industrial consumers revealed that 82 percent of users find this type of information influential. Also, customer testimonials and case studies begin to become popular here, and it is a good idea to use them whenever appropriate.

In the search for supplier stage, consider making a variety of technical videos and product demos to drive home your expertise and offerings for those who are in one of the most intense and crucial stages of the industrial buying cycle.

As this stage progresses, however, you need to break out the big guns—certifications, tolerances, technical specifications, equipment lists, sales drawings, and more. Many technical buyers and engineers require downloadable computer-aided design (CAD) drawings where applicable. If you fail to deliver on this online content, you might end up losing sales.

In the fourth stage, *settle price and select vendor*, aside from paying attention to the customer service and price of your offerings, consider that only the most detailed content and technical information will produce a significant effect here.

In the final stage, *after the sale*, it's important to strengthen branding and marketing messages. Guarantee that buyers have made the right decision improves the chances of repeat business.

Many of the online content that gained merit *before awareness* (advertising and news releases) will come back into play during this fifth, final, and indispensable stage. Thus, make sure you take advantage of social media and e-mail as part of the follow-up process that should become habitual for all "after-sale" activity.

With 64 percent of industrial consumers comparing two or three suppliers before choosing who to ultimately buy from, industrial companies can't underestimate the value of online content in each phase of the sales and marketing strategy.

Providing the right online content to the buyer will increase your likelihood of winning that business, and providing just as much attention and TLC to the after-sale care will help provide for multiple sales and referral sales as well.

Allowing your Prospects to Create their Own Experience: Considering Digital Cocreation

The web is changing the way business is done; many new innovative concepts are becoming available for consumers as they search for a company to meet their industrial business needs. One cutting edge concept in this new world of Internet-based sales is *digital cocreation*.

Digital cocreation is a popular method of product development that brings together businesses and customers in a new, unique way. An online platform where companies and consumers can interact (see below), allows them to collaborate equally, sharing ideas and insights that foster education and cooperation.

This is not solely for the consumer's benefit. Digital cocreation also brings new perspectives to the product development side of your business, letting industrial marketing executives see their products from a consumer point of view.

Digital cocreation enhances the development process and improves ROI in three primary ways:

1. Inexpensive Input from Customers

At the simplest and cheapest level, digital cocreation can consist of a digital survey, e-mailed or distributed through social media networks. However, there are numerous ways for businesses to get creative with customer input.

Shortomatic allows customers to customize their own board shorts—from the legs to the pockets and the trim and much more.

Users pick from a selection of colors, designs, and prints to digitally "cocreate" their own pair of customized board shorts!

This is a great way to please customers—and it lets the company see, for free, which styles and colors they like best. Imagine the R&D savings a digital collaboration like this produces! We can expect to see more customization options like this when marketing for manufacturing companies.

2. Savings on Customer Education and Other Support Activities

When you create products with your customers, you are simultaneously informing them about your company. By taking an active part in product development, they come to know more about the products you offer than if they were to see traditional, one-way, non-interactive advertisements, such as magazine ads or online banners.

With online meeting spaces, such as Shindig.com, hundreds or thousands of participants can be actively involved in an interactive experience. If properly engaged, these people will tell their friends about the fascinating product development they were able to take part in, spreading the word about the business, the products, and the way the customer's opinions are valued as an important part of the process.

3. Savings on Industrial Marketing Expenses

Many cocreation initiatives are highly publicized—and proud of the fact that companies and consumers are contributing to great design. This is especially easy and effective in an online format. This inspires more people to see what all the buzz is about and potentially get involved themselves.

Social media networks provide an unprecedented way to share information, making them fertile ground for industrial marketing or advertising. Users can be found and filtered according to their interests, leading to more efficient, targeted advertising. In addition, friends of these users are often able to see some of their activity, spreading the message even more.

As you begin to get more experienced with LinkedIn, Facebook, Twitter, Pinterest, and other social media sites, you will learn the value of connecting with users in a more one-on-one way.

How Papa John's Combines These Three Tactics Successfully

Papa John's, the famous pizzeria chain, recently made very effective use of Facebook with its "Papa John's Specialty Pizza Challenge." As part of the initiative, they invited users of the popular social media site to submit their own pizza recipes, resulting in more than twelve thousand entries.

Judges, chosen by Papa John's, whittled these thousands of entries down to three finalists: "The Big Bonanza," "The Cheesy Chicken Cordon Bleu," and "The Workin' Fire."

This contest improved Papa John's ROI, using all three of the above principles. For instance, by allowing thousands of Facebook users to design their own pizzas, Papa John's could examine and quantify the tastes of a vast number of people—all for free. By doing so, they also informed thousands more people that they exist and care about the public's tastes in a way that was appealing and interactive. In addition, the process practically marketed itself, as nearly the entire population is plugged into the trends circulating through Facebook.

Using the online collaboration of digital cocreation, Papa John's Pizza saved big money while creating an even bigger presence in the public eye. The industrial world is obviously much different from consumer-based products, but allowing users to define their interactions is an increasingly popular way to customize the online experience for customers. Simplifying the users experience is essential for a successful collaboration.

The Impact of Content Marketing on Industrial Sales

Does the age of digital marketing sound the death knell for traditional salespersons and their several follow-up meetings? It hasn't quite led to the exodus of salespersons many people believed it might, but online marketing *has* radically reduced conventional marketing expenditures. Online marketing includes several components, such as SEO, blogging, PPC, paid advertising, social media, and e-mail marketing.

The Internet has become such a powerful way to advertise that even local brands can attract consumers from all over the world. This has ultimately translated into marketing products and services of international standards.

Globalization is happening aggressively in every industrial sector—with Internet marketing boosting the presence of brands in nearly every corner of the world. But only if it's effective and done right.

- Does your website content match globally recognized standards?
- Are your blogs of a professional-grade quality?
- Does your online marketing rely too heavily on American slang to properly translate across international borders?
- Are you taking international customers into consideration when presenting online marketing materials, such as stock art that is multicultural, etc.?
- Are you merely translating the website content in every language?

If you are still seeking answers to these questions, you need to revise your Internet marketing plan.

Low Traffic and Visibility

Most companies have websites to advertise their services and products on the Internet. However, it is no longer sufficient to just have a website. You must have a website that people see, want to return to, learn something from, and associate with you and your company.

Does your website get enough exposure on the Internet? Are you satisfied with the number of visitors browsing your website? A website with low page rankings on the Internet is practically dead. In this case, Internet marketing tools become indispensable.

Insufficient Content on Blogs and Websites

In the world of Internet marketing, content is king. Search engine results and page rank have an impact on the visibility of the website or blog, but how effective is the actual content on your blog and websites?

SEO used to be king, but Google's algorithm has undergone drastic changes in the last few years. Content writing is no longer restricted to fluffing keywords that would help in SEO. The new search algorithm rewards well-researched, informational content that provides actual information your customers can use.

You Do Not Have Profiles on Social Networking Sites

Do you have an impressive portfolio on LinkedIn? Most professionals from different industries network through LinkedIn to build more social contacts. LinkedIn has millions of users from different industries; not having a profile on this valuable social media site can significantly impact your sales.

Do you have Facebook and Twitter accounts and fan pages for your company? Although, these social media sites are predominantly B2C, branding your manufacturing services on these social networking sites can help drive more traffic to your website and create awareness of your services among consumers.

Three Steps to Boosting Sales through Internet Marketing

The following three steps will help you boost your everyday sales through Internet marketing while reducing the amount of money you spend on direct, more traditional advertising:

Improve the Visibility of Your Website with SEO, SEM, and PPC

The Internet has revolutionized the execution of industrial marketing strategies. Consumers are more aware than ever of new products through online resources and blogs. It is no longer sufficient to create a website for web presence. You can increase the visibility of your website through Internet marketing strategies such as SEO, SEM and PPC.

SEO increases the page rankings of the website through organic search results. Companies can get wider online publicity through SEM. In this case, the visibility of the website is improved through paid inclusion of advertisements. PPC is an important aspect of Internet marketing; the advertiser pays the publisher the requisite rates whenever its ads are clicked.

Create Contacts through Social Media Marketing

Most industries and companies have realized the importance of social media marketing. Facebook, LinkedIn, Twitter, and Google Plus are commonly being used to drive traffic to company websites.

Most companies have accounts and profiles on these social networking sites. This increases their visibility to consumers as manufacturers advertise new product launches and schemes through these social media sites.

Employ Subject Matter Experts to Perform Content Audits

Today's technical buyers are well versed with different products, and you need to curate content to increase its specificity so that yours rises to the top of their radar screens. How do you know which content to provide for your prospects? A content audit by subject matter experts of your company ensures that the online content is mapped to consumers effectively.

Thanks to Internet marketing, industrial companies are witnessing a dramatic surge in sales. The manufacturer channelizes these social media blogs and websites through content marketing. Increasing the visibility of the website translates into attracting more consumers and buyers. This helps them understand the features of products and services at their own pace.

The Competitive Market for Industrial Goods and Services

The desperation in the market for industrial goods and services is almost palpable. The signs are apparent. Staple items sold in the B2B marketplace are continually coming under the assault of downward pricing pressure.

New suppliers rise to take on larger established companies in specialized areas—and disappear in a matter of years from increased competitive tension. Why does this pricing burden seem to intensify as time moves forward? Let's explore the competitive marketplace for industrial goods and services.

Finding Relief in the New

Some companies relieve this pricing pressure in the marketplace by reinventing themselves, their products, and/or their staff. But keeping up a continuous flow of new can drain money, time, and resources away from business as usual. The development of new marketing materials, sales strategies, and training takes time and resources that should be devoted to effective marketing and promotion.

The start-up costs of a new line of business, if implemented too often, eat into a company's profitability. This should cause executives to ask whether a continuous emphasis on the new as a business model is sustainable.

If the industry's niche doesn't support that kind of investment for small businesses, financing new developments may be the incorrect solution for a correctly diagnosed problem.

Needing to Compete on the Basis of Price

Companies that have to respond to the competitive pricing demands of the industry cannot afford to operate under the unrealistic expectation of creating new products to maintain leadership in an industry. When that kind of reaction is necessary, it is likely that the company's prospects and customers were led to the company because they were inexpensive—and not because they provided superior value.

When a company is positioned this way, the only way to increase sales is to lower prices. That strategy works when it done occasionally for a specific business purpose, but when it is a guiding operational principle, financial ruin is probably coming soon. Although marketing on the Internet is competitive, there are better ways to position a company than to compete this way.

Can A Company Have the Wrong Customers?

Price-sensitive clients are likely to be indifferent to the improvements you make, the accessories you add, and the value-added services you provide. If they came for the price, that's likely the only reason they'll stay.

If your goal is to increase profit by providing value that a customer cannot get elsewhere, the customers who purchase from you on the basis of price are the wrong customers. Moreover, they are unlikely to make replacement purchases from you unless your prices are low or comparable. If pricing attracts the wrong kind of client, how can a company attract the right kind?

The Way the Internet *Was* Used to Attract Customers

Successful Internet marketing is driven by a proliferation of strategically designed and carefully placed content. For most of the 2000s, small businesses and marketing consultants focused on placement. As a result, how the content was situated on the Internet mattered most because it drove search rankings.

The conventional wisdom for most of that time was that if a company could attain the most visibility, there would be a direct benefit to their profitability. The logic was that more visibility would lead to more prospects; more prospects would lead to more customers; and more customers would lead to more income and profitability.

This linear formula depended on small businesses and consultants being able to mimic their understanding of search engine formulas for displaying relevant websites. Companies that invested time and resources into knowing how to get their content placed correctly were satisfied that the results they were receiving were maximized. Although it was definitely important, it was of secondary nature to focus on what the content actually said over how it simply ranked during these years.

The Way the Internet *Is* Being Used To Attract Customers

In recent years, marketing practitioners have had to take a more balanced approach as search engine algorithms have grown more difficult to mimic. In fact, according to search engine activity analyst SEOmoz, companies like Google adjust their search engine algorithm approximately five hundred to six hundred times per year. Nobody can keep up. These adjustments have made it more important for businesses to focus on the nature of their content and not just its strategic placement.

It is not enough for content to be considered good reading material. While that may be a nice feature, it's not a necessary one for consumers—and it's not likely to be monetized. Instead, content has to be created with one goal in mind: *to move a prospect at least one step closer to becoming a client.*

That does *not* mean that every single article, video, press release, or podcast needs to have a hard sales message. It means that it needs to leave an impact on the prospect's mind about whether or not they need to do business with a company.

Positioning a Company on the Internet to Find the Right Customers: *USP*

To accomplish this successfully with their content, a company needs to be skilled in utilizing their *unique selling proposition* (USP). The USP explains why a prospect should do business with a particular company.

It is a statement about what sets the company apart from its competitors in one of the following three areas:

- price
- niche or market focus
- something done better than others

With a clear understanding of the USP, all of a company's content will state both directly and indirectly to a potential client why the selling company is the only logical choice for future purchases.

As companies are creating their content for websites, social media, or public relations, it is critical to integrate the understanding of their USP across the board.

In some cases, it may mean reinforcing the chief benefits of working with the firm. In other cases, it will mean discussing the void that is being fulfilled in the marketplace. In still others, it will mean demonstrating specific areas of quality, selection, or service that the firm delivers better than its competition does.

Eight Practical Steps to Crafting the USP

How can you craft an effective USP that will translate to your company and your consumers? The following eight steps will put you in the right direction:

1. Why do people buy from you? If they aren't buying from you, why should they? Survey and interview current and former customers, staff, and management to determine these answers. The most important data (if you don't compete on price) will come from your customers.

2. Once you have this information, determine how you are positioned in the customer's mind, or how you would like to be positioned:
   - Are you the price leader?
   - Do you offer something totally different?
   - Are you niche focused?
   - Are you value focused (i.e. do you provide results that matter to customers)?

3. Analyze your top three competitors. Which of the four positioning categories do they fall into?

4. Make a prioritized list of services or products most desired by your clients.

5. Write the USP in less than a hundred words; why should people do business with you based on the void the competition is not filling?
6. Test the USP in ad copy and website copy—and track the results.
7. Once you have a USP that you would like to use to position yourself, begin to integrate it into all aspects of your promotion.
8. Tweak the USP as necessary.

The most important aspect of integrating the USP is that the context must always truly matter to the reader or prospect. It may be great reading to discuss an industry trend that the company is combating or a new service it is offering. However, if neither of them matter to those who are reading and listening, the content will not accomplish its purpose of moving a prospect closer to becoming a client. Executing on this purpose is vital for any company that wants to be effective in every aspect of the marketing process. Your USP will continue to grow and evolve.

- Does your marketing message matter to customers?
- If so, is it truly unique?
- Does it express *why* customers should come to you?

Don't just write the USP and put it on a shelf; nurture, water, and grow it so it serves you and your company for maximum effect!

PART
4

The Final Conversion—Creating Customers

CHAPTER 13

Creating the Conversion Funnel

Regardless of what types of marketing you use—traditional media or social media, analog or Web 2.0, bulletin boards or Facebook—every sale has a clearly defined process. Part of that process is how prospects are turned—or *converted*—into customers via a "conversion funnel."

A conversion funnel defines the process your website visitors go through from initially clicking on your website to ultimately converting to a purchaser or taking action. It is, in short, a graphical representation of your marketing process.

While it may sound relatively harmless, a conversion funnel can make or break your online industrial marketing campaign. Many things can distract or recruit your website traffic from sticking around to click through to the purchase point; how you approach your conversion funnel is extremely important for turning industrial manufacturing marketing into industrial manufacturing sales.

Properly utilized, a conversion funnel will bring in targeted visitors who are primed, pumped, and ready to make a purchase. An inefficient conversion funnel, on the other hand, will have visitors leaving your website without taking action.

What does the conversion funnel look like? Here are the three phases of the conversion funnel process:

- **Step 1:** Picture a funnel, with the largest part (at the top) being all the visitors coming to your site. How they've gotten there is largely a function of the marketing efforts we've discussed throughout this book. What they do once they arrive at the top of the funnel will largely be dictated by how effectively you convert them.

- **Step 2:** As visitors go through the funnel, reading your product descriptions and sampling demonstration videos, they are pulled farther down with each click of their mouse; eventually they reach the final converters. Not everyone who enters the funnel, naturally, will arrive at the bottom. Your job is to ensure that as many as possible make it to the next step:

- **Step 3:** The final step would be a thank you message after those who made it to the bottom of the conversion funnel actually purchase something.

As you can see, there are as many ways for this process to go right as there are for it to go wrong, making the conversion funnel a critical factor in your marketing efforts.

Why Is a Conversion Funnel Important?

Among other things, a conversion funnel will:

1. **Provide insight into purchasing stages:** If a significant number of prospects leave the conversion funnel at the top, or in the middle, or just before making a purchase, you can pinpoint this step and apply more pressure to ensure that they stick around.

2. **Allow marketing to target visitors:** The conversion funnel, for better or worse, provides the marketing department with a captive audience and the opportunity to target them appropriately.

3. **It can improve conversion rates:** Recognizing the conversion funnel for what it is and learning to master it can improve conversion rates dramatically.

4. **Show areas of marketing strength:** By measuring the number of prospects entering the funnel, how long they stay, and how many actually convert, you can reveal your areas of marketing strength.

5. **Reveal areas of marketing weakness:** Likewise, you can hopefully pinpoint when, and why, prospects opt out before making a purchase.

6. **Play a key role in your marketing for manufacturing:** The more you understand the progress users' chart on the way through your conversion funnel, the more you'll understand how to market your industrial manufacturing firm.

What Causes a Poor Conversion Funnel?

An ineffective conversion funnel can stem from a variety of reasons, but here are the four I've found that consistently cause conversions to fail:

1. **Improperly targeting your market:** If the message on your website is too vague or generic, you may not be able to pull a prospect all the way through the funnel to convert them.

2. **Not knowing your objectives:** If your message is unclear, is all over the place, or strings together keywords and tag lines, prospects will opt out before making a purchase.

3. **Not stimulating your visitors:** If prospects are not stimulated, interested, or able to interact or use features that are quite common elsewhere, such as being able to zoom in or view a product photo from various angles, they may opt out early as well.

4. **Using inactive wording**: Prospects can be led to convert if you use active, engaging text that provides answers and solutions. The opposite will result in lost conversions.

What's The Solution?

The key to having an effective conversion funnel is having strong, clear objectives that make it clear to prospects what solutions you're providing, why, and how. The following questions can help you more clearly define your objective:

- Do you know what you are hoping to accomplish on each page of your website?
- Is the wording clear and active?
- Is the website clean and easy to navigate?
- Do you target your visitors at the most effective time?

In addition to having a clear objective, measurement is a vital part of the conversion process. Therefore, to optimize your conversion funnel, you need to know which metrics to evaluate. To do this, you must dig deep into your site statistics and micro-analyze your sales path to understand what factors might be hindering conversion:

- Where, exactly, are visitors dropping off?
- Which prospects are just browsing?
- Which are ready to take action?

In addition to understanding the strengths and weaknesses of each step of your funnel, you must calculate the drop-off and conversion at every level:

- Do you lack a compelling reason to buy at the product selection stage?
- Do they lose interest due to a confusing process?

How you answer these questions can radically alter the course your potential customers take upon entering the conversion funnel.

How Do You Implement a Solution?

Implementing a solution can be as simple as following the three steps as outlined below:

1.) **Less is (sometimes) more.** You can significantly lower your conversion funnel drop-off rate by decreasing the steps involved. Make it as quick and easy as possible to get those conversions. The fewer steps you have, the more likely people will perform your desired action.

2.) **Call to action.** Optimize your conversion funnel by creating a compelling call to action for every step involved. Make certain each step contains a strong, compelling benefit. Be sure to use action-oriented wording that sparks interest and desire.

3.) **Metrics matter.** Proper measurement can help inform and improve conversion rates. Implement site tracking, such as Google Analytics, to properly analyze the pages of your site. This allows you to track goal funnels and view page visitors, and it plays a role in optimizing your sales.

Improving Your Website Conversion Rate

Website conversion rate is the term used to define the process of converting your visitors from passive readers to action-taking people. Not surprisingly, it is a critical part of the overall sales funnel for industrial marketing electronically.

Having a better website conversion rate does not mean you are above your competition—it means you are effectively meeting your industrial marketing objectives.

There is a kind of organic momentum to your web conversion rate. The more successful your web conversion rate, the more popular your industrial marketing site will be to visitors and other sites, increasing your link exchange and, inevitably, the amount of website visitors who enter your conversion funnel.

The search engines love links and will bring more traffic to your site; the more attractive and full of resources and solutions your site is, the more traffic you'll convert to sales.

The problem with website conversion rate is that not everyone understands how to do it properly. The necessary tools are not in place—or the objectives are unclear or not being implemented properly.

Your website conversion rate may be lower than anticipated due to a variety of other specific factors:

1.) **Visitors do not trust you or your site.** For whatever reason, they feel uncomfortable doing business with you. Having clear objectives and offering solutions instead of sales copy can help build trust among uncertain users.

2.) **Visitors have concerns about your products, services, or other offerings.** This may be a result of poorly written—or inactively written—product descriptions, not enough information, too much of the wrong (sales type) information, or other factors that require closer study and analysis to rectify.

3.) **Your site is not user-friendly.** This one is a biggie. If your site causes more confusion and frustration than desired, or is necessary, you will definitely see a drop in your conversion rate. Users like simplicity; less is more.

You've seen what might adversely affect your conversation rate, but where do you start when it comes to making improvements? There are a number of things you can do to improve your website conversion rate.

1.) **Utilize a number of trust factors throughout your pages.** Visitors must feel comfortable with you and your company before they commit to a purchase.

2.) **Develop a variety of useful tools that enhance your industrial marketing merchandising.** Simple things, from a web-design standpoint—allowing visitors to zoom in for a better look at your product descriptions, ask questions in a forum, or chat with a sales rep—can greatly enhance your conversion rate.

3.) **Make your website as user-friendly as possible to enhance your visitor's experience.** Slow loading, auto-starting animation or sounds, broken links, or too many links can drive prospects away from your site. View your web design and functionality from a consumer's perspective to strip it down to pure functionality over how pretty it is or how many bells and whistles you can cram onto each page.

4.) **Analyze each page and determine which is meeting your objectives and which is not.** Again, look at each page from a consumer's perspective to properly analyze it for clear, solution-providing objectives.

5.) **Know what your objectives are.** What action do you want your visitors to take? Do you want subscriptions? Product purchases? Appointments? Once you know your industrial marketing objectives, you can implement behavioral targeting.

Implementing a Solution in Five Simple Steps

In order to ensure that you are working at peak conversation status, I offer the following five-step solution:

1. **Industrial marketing means you must focus on your trust factors.** Display third-party accreditation on your home page and throughout your site. Clearly list your

terms and conditions. Develop a "contact us" page and reveal your physical address, phone number, fax number, and other pertinent information.

2. **Marketing for manufacturing means staying current with your merchandising offers.** Use price competitiveness and product relevancy, introduce irresistible product offers, utilize clear product descriptions, consider free delivery to increase conversion rate, maintain proper inventory, and use images.

3. **Develop a user-friendly site by avoiding mistakes, such as poor grammar, spelling, and punctuation.** Make certain your links operate. Be sure your pages download quickly. Test each sales step in your conversion funnel.

4. **Start using a "multivariate testing" tool, such as Google Website Optimizer, to simultaneously test numerous variables.** You can determine which images and pages draw attention, which headings work, and other relevant information.

5. **Use behavioral targeting to improve your website conversion rate.** Analyze your page data to determine where to place targeted and relevant ads at optimum times throughout the call-to-action process.

Five Ways Industrial Businesses Can Use Online Videos to Convert

Have you thought of adding videos to your website to increase your conversation rate? Statistics from the 2012 Social Media Marketing Industry Report revealed that 76 percent of businesses plan on increasing their use of online video, such as YouTube, and video marketing, making it a top area that most industrial marketing professionals will invest in for 2012.

Even more interesting is that businesses with 26-999 employees indicated this is a key growth area, with at least 80 percent responding positively. Younger marketers (77 percent of those aged 20-49) are also more likely to raise their video production than older marketers (68 percent of those older than sixty).

While these are among the most common uses of video marketing, there are other ways to use online videos as part of your sales and marketing conversion strategies. Specifically, here are five uses for online videos that you may not have thought of. Each video should always lead prospective customers into the next stage of the conversion cycle.

Show How Products Are Manufactured

Rather than showing how a particular product works, industrial companies can demonstrate the process of manufacturing their products. In fact, the survey reported that 82 percent of buyers prefer to read detailed product descriptions before making a purchase. These types of videos can go beyond listing tolerances and specifications by revealing the process of manufacturing.

Custom manufacturers can make similar videos that feature the production process of custom components from their portfolio. According to the latest survey, patrons of custom manufacturing usually look for information on a supplier's expertise/specializations (74 percent) and capabilities and applications (69 percent), which such online videos can satisfy.

Inform about the Life Cycle of a Product

Getting more specific about your products can get you more sales. For instance, industrial companies can provide valuable information about the product's life expectancy, maintenance, and proper disposal procedures, as well as how to find out if a product is beyond refurbishing or repair, and possible post-life applications, such as material recycling. This also provides the chance to discuss warranty program offerings, maintenance, and replacement.

Educate Buyers about Your Industry

Technical buyers are sometimes well versed in the kinds of services and products they source. Here are some simple tips on how you can educate potential buyers in your industry:

- Make a guide video about your products/services that non-technical buyers can understand, yet which conveys vital information that helps buyers make the right choice.
- Be sure to include relevant information that explains the factors that make your products and services unique. This will ease the way into a technical call, which potentially speeds up the buying process. Also, it demonstrates technical expertise and places your company as experts in the services or products you offer.

Profile Superstar Employees

A business is only as good as its workforce. Show the integrity of your company with a short video that features some of your best employees. Interviewing workers who have a great influence on the product—such as machinists and engineers—demonstrates your consistency, quality, and reliability.

Moreover, showcase your customer service by featuring technical sales representatives and CSRs. This will help new clients get to know more about your company, and it's a great way to develop morale.

Showcase Eco-Friendly Efforts or Community Outreach

You may consider one of these for your videos. They are all in the same category and convey dedication and responsibility. Although corporate social responsibility has decreased in the past few years, these programs continue to affect your company's reputation in a positive way.

The Long Tail: *Why Faster Isn't Always Better*

Conversion takes time, and the work you're doing today often takes several tomorrows before it pays fruit. In fact, the sales process for B2B marketing can be long and tortuous before funds are actually disbursed or checks are signed. A prospect becoming a customer typically doesn't happen with one visit to your site or plant. It is likely to happen over the course of a number of discussions, analyses, or collaborations. Since the dollar amounts are larger than most average B2C transactions, companies must be willing to work with these inefficiencies in the sales process.

However, a company's expenses aren't afforded the same inefficiencies. Raw materials must be purchased, utility bills must be paid, and loan payments must be remitted. Delays in making payments can cause higher rates, higher fees, and less friendly future terms.

Companies that are able to work through the sales process quickly avoid the negative consequences associated with a minimal amount of cash flow. Companies that successfully manage cash flow are able to take advantage of more favorable terms, rates, and fees. In many cases, they are able to use excess cash to minimize lending costs.

Moving Through the Sales Cycle: *Funneling Down in Four Simple Steps*

As we near the end of our discussion on the conversion funnel, consider a few more questions:

- If there are advantages to moving customers through an industrial marketing funnel faster, what can companies do to increase the speed of a transaction?

169

- Does marketing for manufacturing automatically mean an excruciatingly slow process?
- Are there tools and strategies that industrial marketers can use to increase the workflow and productivity of the sales process without jeopardizing the customer relationship?

Marketing for manufacturing necessitates many conversations and visits, but most of this is a convincing process and relationship-building process. The key to speeding up the workflow can be expressed in the three following strategies:

- build relationships with prospects before there is anything to sell;
- open up opportunities for two-way dialogues with prospects before there is anything to sell
- provide as much expert information about industry problems and solutions as possible

Exercising these principles on a regular basis can help a company's management of its prospect relationships. Companies can take certain practical steps to accomplish these objectives.

1. **Webinars work.** Companies should invite customers and prospects to free online conferences (webinars) and invite their feedback on the subject matter. This will give prospects familiarity with the company, its philosophy, and its expertise.
2. **Build your (video) backlog.** Companies can create an exhaustive YouTube video library to answer industry problems, demonstrate products and services, and share research findings. This will give prospects familiarity with the company's expertise as well as its product and service line.
3. **Invitation only.** Companies can create closed social media groups to discuss real-time issues as they occur. This social aspect of contact will familiarize management to prospects.

4. **Popular podcasts.** Companies can create podcasts of management discussing industry trends. As is the case with other aspects of creating conversation, a podcast is an opportunity to hear a dynamic two-way conversation between two people from the same company.

Parting Words about the Conversion Funnel

The best way to expedite the sales process is to give clients more opportunities to meet and get to know management. Industrial marketing still comes back to the relationships between the customers disbursing funds and the companies receiving them.

The more comfortable a client is with the expertise of a company for solving industry problems, the less the process of closing prospects will be drawn out. Are your clients and prospects familiar with your level of expertise? What are you doing to let them know? The more solutions, knowledge, and expertise you can offer your prospects, the sooner they'll convert to customers.

CHAPTER 14

Effective Calls to Action

Part of finding success in industrial marketing depends on putting yourself in your customer's shoes. Who are they? Where are they? Why do they ultimately choose you? Those are the questions we've been struggling to answer throughout this book. Another important question is *where* they should go to find you?

Increasingly, they go online. Industrial companies use the Internet as an instrument for research, online sourcing, and procurement. This greatly favors sales of industrial products because industrial businesses manufacture costly goods that were routinely researched before purchase—even before the web.

Costly purchases require careful consideration and budgeting, which is a process that is greatly facilitated by Internet access. As we've discussed thoroughly, the creation of content is designed to draw attention to your products.

Studies show that more than 50 percent of all consumers turn to the Internet to obtain the information they need to make cost-effective sourcing and procurement decisions. This provides a great opportunity for industrial companies to develop strategies for optimal placement, promotion, and sale of their products.

It is important for industrial companies to have their products easily found online, but having products showcased on your company's website is not enough to secure adequate sales. A well-crafted user experience makes your website more effective in sales conversions.

Employing best practices in tailoring the online user experience is an essential part of converting leads into sales. One such best practice that can be easily implemented is the call to action (CTA). This chapter discusses what a CTA is, how it works, why it works, and details the best practices that can help industrial companies create more effective CTAs.

What Is a Call to Action?

The CTA is a set of instructions and information given to the consumer to seal the deal. Ultimately, the CTA empowers your business to control your sales process and increase its sales.

Everyone is familiar with the generic instruction that says "click here," while it may be an action, it is not a call to action. A call to action is not a single action in the complex sales process; it is a sophisticated series of incentives and instructions designed to result in a specific user behavior that is desired by the company and consented to by the user.

Crafting the Call to Action: *Three Elements No CTA Can Do Without*

The call to action is, first and foremost, a carefully crafted strategy to increase leads and sales. It systematically educates the user about what you have to offer and why your offer will benefit them.

Effective calls to action don't just happen by accident. In fact, a key part of creating an effective call to action is to make it concise, precise, and consistent.

- **Concise:** When it comes to crafting an effective CTA, less is often more. Being concise is important because it cuts down on confusion and distractions that could pull the user's attention away from the CTA.

- **Precise:** Be clear, focused, and precise. Being precise increases the chances that the user understands exactly what is to be done, which reduces errors.
- **Consistent:** Unlike a single message or even action, like "click here," your CTA is a lively network or collection of messages, inducements, and instructions that link to each other to be effective. Using language that is consistent is important because the call to action involves more than one web page.

Like a matching color scheme that flows through a house, the CTA isn't just one sales page with an order form; it is a series of steps spread across your entire web universe.

The action may begin on a web page or within an e-mail, but it continues on another page (the landing page). The CTA can conclude on the landing page, but a third page involving payment for a service or product may be involved.

An Optimal CTA

As sophisticated as they can get, a call to action still only has two basic steps:

- presentation of the CTA
- transfer to the landing page

Of course, a lot happens between these two steps to get web users to consumers, and I'll dig deeper into each of these in this chapter.

Presentation of the CTA

The first step in the presentation of the CTA is to establish what action(s) you want to take place, such as signing up for a newsletter, purchasing a product, or downloading a white paper.

An incentive is typically used to let the user know that completing the action will have a value-added outcome. The incentive should be relevant to your niche. It should state clearly and precisely what is being offered—and tell the user why the offer benefits them.

Design Elements and Other Qualities of an Optimal CTA

More than just words, a good call to action has several additional qualities that should be demonstrated in the content and design for your CTA. In order to optimize your CTA, you should:

- **Use Action Words That Convey Urgency:** An optimal CTA conveys a sense of urgency and gives a compelling reason why action should be taken now—not later. Remember to use the same philosophy with individual words that you use with your overall CTA message: *concise, precise* and *consistent*.
- **Select Optimal Color and Positioning for Your CTA Button/Hyperlink:** Graphics, as well as words, are an integral part of your CTA. Specifically, the CTA should be embodied by a visual cue, such as a hyperlink or button. Best practices should be applied to the design of the CTA button or link and how it is positioned on the page. Best visual practices that apply to the CTA are:

  o The link or button should be surrounded by white space so that the cue is visualized, and no other graphics or statements compete for the user's attention.
  o Use concise wording, easily read fonts, color, and layout to increase the efficacy of your CTA button or hyperlink. Orange is said to be the "perfect color" for a CTA button because it conveys urgency and is also playful. Red is not the best

choice because it has negative associations, such as debt and danger. Green is another good color because people find it visually pleasing. Blue can work against you because it favors caution and may cause the user to reconsider—often at the most crucial step in the buying process.

o   The CTA button should be large enough to stand out on the page. Using a large font on the button can help it stand out. According to *Smashing* magazine, positioning the CTA button in the top half of the web page increases landing page conversions.

- **Prioritize If You Have More Than One CTA**: If you have more than one CTA, you should prioritize whichever is more important. The CTA button for the most important call can be bigger or a brighter color can make it stand out. Each page should focus on *one* major call to action dedicated to success.

Tell the User Know Exactly What to Expect

Above all, when it comes to your CTA, the user should know *exactly* what will happen when they click on the link or button. (If your wording has been concise, precise, and consistent, that shouldn't be a problem!)

For instance, if the offer is free, say so. Tell the user if the download is going to take up 35 MB of space on their hard drive before they click on the button. Being upfront and accurate about what is going to happen will help users trust you.

Examples of common CTAs are:

- "Download our Free White Paper Now!"
- "Call us for your Free Quote."
- "Download the Product Comparison Now!"
- "Instant Spec Download."

Case Study # 1: Lowe's

Lowe's, the company that has specialized in Do-It-Yourself supplies for decades, has several CTAs throughout its website (Lowes.com), all maintaining a consistent color scheme and appeal. When visiting the Lowe's building supplies page, you can see instantly the CTA in the main image at the top, which rotates through a series of images.

Concise use of the call to action is visible. There is little hesitation on what Lowes.com wants their visitors to do when they arrive on the building supplies page. The CTA is clearly visible and pops out by using a vibrant, yet not overwhelming, green button to encourage the user to take action.

Precise use of the call to action is always used. There is little doubt what you're getting from the text on each call to action used with concise, precise, and consistent messages such as:

- Shop Decking
- Save on Ceiling Tiles
- Shop DIY Project Kits

I am certain you have a clear understanding of where you are heading when you click on those actions. Consistency is a big focus throughout the entire website, driving home the message in a uniform, enthusiastic way. What's nice about effective CTAs is that, even if you don't act your first time on the website, you will find the same conciseness, preciseness, and consistency the next time—and every time—you visit.

Case Study # 2: IndustrialSupplies.com

IndustrialSupplies.com, a leading supplier of industrial materials and supplies, has put the CTA to work in a big way on their website. From the homepage on, you are greeted with a consistent use of color, text, and graphics that guide the user's experience in the way they choose.

The common use of spot colors (consistent use of colors to guide the eye path) is done in a remarkable manner that leaves you no choice but to follow the path. Arrows are a big part of the overall thematic design of the site itself, leaving no question about which direction they want you to take.

From the moment you arrive on the website, you have no other option than to follow the motions. I particularly like how effectively the website uses the concise, precise, and consistent model so well.

- **Concise:** From the top of the page down, your eye is led from section to section of the site, each displaying a new focal point. Although the path may be a bit distracting to focus on one call to action, the company uses a bright yellow color to guide and ensure the user focuses on what they feel is important. There is also a simplicity to the site; a few prominent boxes call for your attention, but there is little else to distract you from priority items.

- **Precise:** "Free Shipping," "Shop Now," "Everything You Need for Your Business," whichever message you respond to the most, you'll have a tough time not finding *something* that will appeal to you on this website. Each call to action has a specific action that they want the user to follow. More specified action could hold an argument here; however, due to the volume of products, the company has the unique opportunity to highlight multiple opportunities for a wide variety of user groups.

- **Consistency:** Perhaps the most effective point of their CTAs is the fact that they use the same spot color to make many calls to action easy to navigate through. The main reason this website doesn't overwhelm its users is because there is a consistent pattern between the use of color in text and graphics that allows its many messages to be non-invasive to the user. They stand out in a way that makes navigation easy and beneficial to its user.

CTA Optimization Increases Sales Conversions

Effective CTAs don't just pay off—they payoff big! According to Marketingexperiments.com, optimization of the page containing your CTA by using an uncluttered layout, action-oriented headers, optimized buttons/links, and a winning value-added offer can increase your click-through rate by "as much as 266 percent," and your conversion rate by "as much as 26 percent."

The key is to strike the balance, as the Lowe's and IndustrialSupplies.com websites do, between action and distraction. Companies often take the "more is more" approach to CTAs, littering their websites, blogs, and online catalogs with so many CTAs—or so many images broadcasting their CTAs—that potential buyers leave too soon and purchase too rarely.

Calls to Action: How to Effectively Use Them in Social Media

Calls to action are the cherry on top of a well-built sundae. Without them, the magical sales pitch doesn't quite have the effect that the sales pitcher wants to achieve.

Although some might believe the classic print call to action works best and use calls to action in social media the same way, social media requires a much simpler—and unique—approach.

Just as in every form of marketing, there is usually no one-size-fits-all approach. In social media, all you want the reader to do is click on the link, which means a simple, direct, last word-style call to action works best.

Poorly placed calls to action result in low conversion, even in social media where all you need the reader to do is click the link. The location or quality of the call to action might not be to blame; the rest of the pitch has to connect with the reader and make them want to learn more.

A well-written pitch can still be turned on its head with a misplaced call to action that blunts the message and sends the reader someplace else for conciseness, preciseness, and consistency.

Without an effectively placed call to action, the sale pitch falls flat. On Twitter, the call to action might take up one-third of the allotted space.

The call to action becomes even more important and essential in social media. All effective social media calls to action meet the following criteria:

- **Inspire action.** Regardless of the medium, the call to action should encourage the reader to act. Social media makes up the top of your sales funnel. You want them to click on the link and continue to the next part of the funnel. Most calls to action have a strong verb like "tweet this" or "click to read more." Of course, it's possible not to have a verb at all.
- **Be direct.** Don't beat around the bush or lead them on. You want the reader to do something; the most effective way is to say it concisely.
- **Give back.** When the reader clicks the link, they should receive something for their efforts—like additional information or warm, fuzzy feelings from sharing the information with others.
- **Located last.** Calls to action most often come at the end of the social media post. Think of the preceding text as a short introduction or paragraph-long sales pitch. It should be the last thing read by the reader, so they click the link.
- **Don't just "sell, sell, sell."** It's tempting to oversell in social media, but your followers will just remove your business from their list of companies they follow. Instead, follow the tips above to craft more effective CTAs.

Examples of Calls to Action for Social Media

- Same-Day Catalog + 20 Percent Off (Follow with a link.)
- Like Us on Facebook and Get Free Shipping.

- 20 Percent Off Next Twenty-Four Hours (Follow with a link to online store)
- Retweet for a Chance to Win

In comparison, print calls to action look like the ones below. Keep in mind that calls to action like these won't work for social media, and what works in social media generally will not work in print. In essence, the examples below are what not to do when crafting social media CTAs. There are easier ways to get them to take advantage of the offer.

Web Call to Action Examples

- Fill out the Form for Instant Access
- Start a Free Trial Today
- Receive Free Samples Today
- Order by the 15th and Get Free Shipping

Social media calls to action use similar concepts as their print predecessors, but the short, conversation style of social media has forced them to be shorter to inspire action in the moment.

Parting Words about Your Call to Action

Industrial companies manufacture products that are costly and subject to comparison pricing. Use of the Internet to facilitate purchasing decisions is a dominant marketing trend that is unlikely to be reversed; therefore, it is beneficial for industrial companies to proactively manage their Internet presence to optimize sales efficacy.

Skillful use of best practices for the creation of effective CTAs can help industrial companies maximize use of their websites, increase lead generation, and drive sales.

CHAPTER **15**

Landing with Impact

When all is said and done, you are not in business to market your industrial products, but to sell them. Picture the conversion tunnel as a series of events leading up to a potential sale; your landing page is the finish line where a prospect finally closes the deal and commits to a purchase.

The Landing Page

As the name implies, your landing page gives details about how and why your proposition has value to your buyers. The ultimate purpose of the landing page is to close the sale or complete the action for which the page was designed. It is where the prospect finds the final validation he or she needs to click "buy" or leave the page—and the transaction—altogether.

Your content needs to set your offer apart from any others the prospect is entertaining. Writing excellent copy for your landing page will increase the chances that the user will stay on the page long enough to fill out the form or complete whatever actions are necessary to bring the offer to a conclusion.

How much time do you have to sway a customer? Not much! According to HubSpot, you have *three seconds* to orient a visitor to your landing page. If they are unable to get what the page is about, they will leave—and not look back.

Using best practices will increase the efficacy for your landing pages.

- **Use action verbs and action-oriented phrases.** Look at your favorite e-tail websites for how they phrase their landing pages. Phrases like "Download Now," "Get Started," "Get It Now," "Ship for Free," and "Try Before You Buy" help prospects sit up and pay attention.

- **Use the second person when creating landing page content.** Use of "you" and "your" creates the sense that you are talking directly to the user in a friendly voice. This is conducive to trust.

- **Use reader keywords.** While it may sound similar, it is different from search engine keywords. "Reader keywords" confirm that the landing page is the fulfillment of the offer in the initial CTA. If the CTA promised a download of a white paper about best business practices, reiterate that on the landing page. The language in the content from the page the user has left should blend logically with the landing page. Dissimilarities will lead the user to suspect a bait-and-switch tactic—and make them leave.

- **Focus on clarity of communication.** Simplicity is better than frills. Frills can be distracting. Make it strong, active, and beneficial; above all, make the message clear. Tell them what they are getting—in the most compelling *and* clearest way possible.

- **Make the content easy on the eyes.** When it comes to landing pages, less really *is* more. Keep copy to five lines or less. Format the content using headers or subtitles that progress logically and grab the user's attention. These "road signs" drive the users where you want them to go. Finally, use • bullet points and **bold fonts** or <u>underline</u> important points to make them stand out.

- **Proofread your content to check for brevity and clarity.** It may help to read the content out loud for additional perspective. Peer review is also good; having another person proof the content with a fresh pair of eyes can be helpful (especially if they've been uninvolved with the rest of the creative process).

Since landing pages increase sales conversions, it is logical to assert that every CTA should have its own landing page. Over time, the content of the landing page can be changed and studied to see which version yields the best conversion rates.

Creating Landing Pages That Convert: Ten Steps for Success

Years ago, online marketers agonized constantly over developing the right portals for their company home pages. Back then, when most web surfers typed in URLs based on key phrases or brand names, you could focus an audience on one or two critical paths. Today, thanks to online advertising and deep links on search engine results, many of your site's visitors won't even see your home page until after a few clicks.

The most effective landing pages—and why would you settle for anything less?—focus your prospects' attention, turning them from curious into paying customers.

When you build additional landing pages for different stages of your audience's buying cycle, you can leverage that trust and generate repeat business.

Based on the wisdom of the industry's most influential designers and marketers, the following steps can help turn your company's landing pages into powerful loyalty engines and help you "land with impact" every time:

1.) Define your conversion goals.

You can't measure success until you define it. Getting clear about your vision of success will shape how you build a landing page and, more specifically, your goals for its design. For instance, an e-commerce site defines conversion as "closing a sale without the user stepping through intermediate pages."

Is your goal more immediate? "Buy now" means the money's in your bank account, and the product is on its way to the customer. You'll use more direct language and sales tactics on this kind of landing page, but only if you're clear on your goals before the design phase begins.

On the other hand, a lead-generation page for a service company might have an easier time getting visitors to request a quote or a contact since the buying will be much more personalized for them.

Conversion, in this case, might mean achieving a filtered number of qualified leads—prospects who meet specific income or decision-making guidelines. The language, images, and design you use on the page should draw in your target audience without causing distractions for your sales team.

2.) Stretch your conversion funnel.

Novice marketers often assume that the right sales letter or the perfect promotional image will convert a browser into a buyer within a single visit. While that feat is not entirely unprecedented, most of us tend to visit sites a few times before we decide to make a purchase.

The idea of the conversion funnel isn't necessarily to rush folks through; instead, design a "web" of quality content and insistence that will encourage them to return several times until, at last, they "land with impact" and decide to purchase. Instead of worrying about closing the deal in one click, build a landing page that moves your prospect one closer to your goal.

According to SEO expert and marketing pundit Bruce Clay, you should minimize the number of intermediate steps your prospects take before completing a sale. Depending on your business, this could mean one extra step—or up to a dozen. How will you know how many steps are right for you? Through careful testing and analysis, you can learn how to tighten your sales cycle.

A typical landing page conversion funnel for a manufacturer might look something like this:

- landing page from a search engine advertisement, promoting a free newsletter
- a newsletter issue with a call to action, promoting a free white paper
- landing page for the white paper signup, offering a free quote or consultation
- final landing page to confirm the quote and complete the transaction

Each step in the funnel should contain a clear call to action, driving the prospect forward without distraction. You can measure overall conversion from start to finish while tweaking the interim steps to improve your success rate and lead more folks to the landing page.

3.) Find your brand voice.

In the early days of radio, stage performers visualized themselves communicating through sheets of gauze to exaggerate their personalities for the new medium.

Your landing pages aren't much different. They are the "best" of your brand on display for all to see, and they must communicate your brand effectively and in a way that is unique to you as a company, CEO, or marketing department.

Psychologists estimate that we make our minds up about first impressions literally "in the blink of an eye." Therefore, the language and imagery you select for your landing page immediately and, for most users, indelibly set the tone for your future customer relationships. Many companies have found their brand voice early and made it work for them.

Dollar Shave Club's founders burned out on clichéd consumer packaged goods marketing. Their frustration spawned one of the web's biggest subscription sales success stories. With brash language, crisp design, and a goofy video, their landing pages appeal to men who value simplicity and savings.

TapTapTap launched their successful Camera + iPhone application with a series of landing pages that blended professional photos with video from cofounder Lisa Bettany. The pages' smooth design echoed the aspirations of an audience that craves more sophistication than the standard camera app.

4.) Build on a solid platform.

You don't have to code landing pages by hand. In fact, many popular content management systems include tools that automatically generate multiple versions of landing pages that you can customize based on your audience, your advertising, or even your offer.

Programmers using Adobe's popular Dreamweaver tool can use the software's template system to build variations of the same HTML layout. WordPress and Drupal offer database-driven alternatives that can even rotate offers on demand.

Regardless of the platform you use, an effective landing page strategy requires constant testing and innovation to ensure that it is accomplishing your primary goals.

As we've seen throughout this book, modern users demand interactivity and ingenuity to meet their web-browsing needs. Don't expect to post a single landing page and wait for the leads to come rolling in.

Google's Website Optimizer and other automated testing tools measure the effectiveness of your copy, layout, and page elements. You can subscribe to site-building and hosting services that manage the entire process of generating and testing alternate versions of your landing pages.

5.) Use clear headlines and quality writing.

The largest words on your landing page should echo the call to action that brought a visitor to your site in the first place. Research shows that interest in landing pages drops off significantly when users feel hijacked by a content bait and switch that promised one thing and offered something else.

Deliver on the promise you made in your ads, newsletters, or social media posts—or promise something else. Short-term gains from bait-and-switch tactics rarely result in customer loyalty; it can backfire in this day and age of transparent social media.

Likewise, many of your site's visitors will abandon your conversion funnel when you post misspelled words or use phrases with poor grammar. Despite society's acceptance of casual e-mail and crazy text message spelling, typos on your landing pages will tarnish your brand.

To ensure that you create content that is actionable and not laughable—or counterproductive—hire a professional commercial copywriter to build, or at least edit, the words you include on your landing pages.

6.) Get visual.

According to researchers at ColorMatters.com, the colors you pick for your landing pages can impact your conversion. We touched on this in the previous chapter, but as a general guide:

- *Blue* pages evoke security and trust.
- *Green* pages usually denote wealth or abundance.
- *Orange* elements grab attention.
- *Purple* pages perform well with beauty products.
- *Black* pages work best for luxury brands.

Some colors only lend themselves to specific purposes. While we associate red with power and urgency, marketers have found that consumers often associate the color with overused discount

promotions. A sparing use of red can draw attention to a limited time offer, but an entire page of red can scare buyers away.

As with everything else about your landing page, don't be afraid to experiment with different versions, designs, templates, and color schemes until you find the most effective combination.

7.) Contrast targeted audiences.

In your own conversations, you've probably noted that the tone of your voice changes according to the situation—low and quiet for a serious discussion, high and animated when you are excited. The language of your landing page should be no different.

In fact, branding expert Matt Peters notes that you should consider variations of your brand voice for different situations. A landing page you advertise on a blog for new parents shouldn't sound the same as a landing page promoted on a hockey news website. Both pages can be equally effective and persuasive—but only if they remain authentic to your brand and your audience.

Don't go overboard, though. Ren Walker writes that some designers fall back on simple stereotypes when trying to build landing pages that appeal to women. Instead of building a pink version of your site for women, try using more white space and fewer closed-off elements.

8.) Keep it brief and to the point.

Despite the presence of scroll bars on all major web browsers, smartphones, and tablets, many people still like to make up their mind about landing pages based on what they see "above the fold."

The headline of your CTA should be visible at the top of the landing page, the first thing new visitors see—without needing to scroll down to find the "special offer" or "buy" button.

Therefore, keep key images and at least one call to action on your landing page's first screen. Developers at 37signals discovered that limiting their landing page to a single screen with no scroll significantly increased the number of signups to their Highrise CRM application.

If you prefer the tone of a long sales letter that builds tension and tells a complex story, break your content into manageable chunks that take up about a screen each. Use subheads, graphic dividers, or contrasting color backgrounds to divide the sections of your landing page.

Modern CSS elements let you have fun with sliding backgrounds and other playful storytelling elements. Use a call to action in each segment so visitors can drive the experience.

9.) Highlight social proof—and then request feedback.

Burned out on scams and empty promises, modern online audiences now demand to know whether they'll get what they expect when they complete your call to action. Showing social proof—evidence that other people enjoy the same products or services and tout them highly—builds the kind of trust you need to convince your prospects to move further through your marketing funnel.

Here are some forms of social proof:

- faces of Facebook friends who completed the same call to action
- testimonials from satisfied customers
- endorsements from trusted advisors
- awards, reviews, and other validations from independent third parties
- tallies of units sold or subscriptions confirmed

A user of a popular newsletter management tool, who's name we'll leave out for now as we couldn't get an okay to include them here, tested versions of a landing page with and without the number of subscribers. The version featuring the social proof that others had subscribed converted *more than 30 percent better* than the version that failed to disclose an audience statistic to build user trust.

10.) Keep innovating.

Always. Be. Innovating!

Because technology keeps evolving, be prepared to keep testing your landing pages for potential improvements and enhancements.

- Plan on responding to new competitors, along with changes in market conditions that can affect your audience.
- Set a time each week, each month, and each quarter to review your analytics for important trends.
- Reset landing pages that don't convert consistently—even as you add experimental landing pages that test new ideas.
- Let statistics guide your decisions, emphasizing actual customer actions over feedback from a few of your loudest audience members.

Lastly, keep an open mind. Keep searching for new ideas—from competitors or websites in other industries that still have effective calls to action or landing pages worth emulating. Don't be afraid to borrow inspiration from a variety of sources in order to finesse your landing page. After all, you never know when—or where—inspiration may strike!

Parting Words about Landing with Impact

With these steps in mind, you can now start building landing pages that grow your customer base without resorting to sneaky tactics.

What's more, you can have a template in place for future landing pages so that you don't have to reinvent the wheel each time. As you become more and more comfortable "landing with impact," the process will become easier—and more effective.

CPSIA information can be obtained at www.ICGtesting.com
Printed in the USA
LVOW04s0515181114

414166LV00012B/221/P

9 781475 998474